PENGUIN BOOKS

smart
food

Jane Barnes is a consultant nutritionist and nutrition communicator, dietitian and author; her other books include *The Healthy Revolution Cookbook* and *Healthy Eating on a Budget*.

Syd Pemberton is a food consultant, caterer, educator and author; her other books include the *Pocket Soup Cookbook*, *Pocket Cakes and Puddings Cookbook*, *Pocket Wok Cookbook*, *Pocket Muffin Book*, *How to Clean Practically Anything*, *Kitchen Wizardry & Household Lore* and *Syd Pemberton's Ecologically Sound Household Handbook*.

Jane Barnes and Syd Pemberton's first project together was *High-Calcium Cooking*, published by Viking in 1999.

GW00633322

smart food

JANE BARNES & SYD PEMBERTON

PENGUIN BOOKS

Penguin Books Australia Ltd
487 Maroondah Highway, PO Box 257
Ringwood, Victoria 3134, Australia
Penguin Books Ltd
Harmondsworth, Middlesex, England
Penguin Putnam Inc.
375 Hudson Street, New York, New York 10014, USA
Penguin Books Canada Limited
10 Alcorn Avenue, Toronto, Ontario, Canada M4V 3B2
Penguin Books (NZ) Ltd
Cnr Rosedale and Airborne Roads, Albany, Auckland, New Zealand
Penguin Books (South Africa) (Pty) Ltd
5 Watkins Street, Denver Ext 4, 2094, South Africa
Penguin Books India (P) Ltd
11, Community Centre, Panchsheel Park, New Delhi 110 017, India

First published by Penguin Books Australia 2001

10 9 8 7 6 5 4 3 2 1

Copyright © Jane Barnes & Syd Pemberton, 2001

The moral right of the authors has been asserted

All rights reserved. Without limiting the rights under copyright reserved above,
no part of this publication may be reproduced, stored in or introduced into a
retrieval system, or transmitted, in any form or by any means (electronic,
mechanical, photocopying, recording or otherwise), without the prior written
permission of both the copyright owner and the above publisher of this book.

Design by Tony Palmer, Penguin Design Studio
Photography by Julie Anne Renouf, styling by Maureen McKeown
Typeset in 10.5/14 pt Berkeley by Midland Typesetters, Maryborough, Victoria
Printed and bound in Australia by Australian Print Group, Maryborough, Victoria

National Library of Australia
Cataloguing-in-Publication data:

Barnes, Jane A.
Smart food.

ISBN 0 14 100736 2.

1. Cookery. I. Pemberton, Syd. II. Title.

641.563

www.penguin.com.au

contents

Introduction: Smart eating   1

Snacks, appetisers & dips   15
Soups & sandwiches   25
Salads   37
Pasta & pizza   51
Rice & couscous   61
Vegetarian mains   77
Fish & seafood   95
Meat & poultry   109
Desserts & baking   135

Index   159

introduction: smart eating

food for living

When we lived off the land, eating was less complicated: you grabbed whatever food you could and were thankful that your belly was full; the healthy result was that you escaped starvation and lived to see another day! Today, the ready availability of nutritious foods, combined with the diversity and complexity of our food supply, raise issues beyond mere survival. We now know that what we eat affects our health and energy, both immediately and longer-term, but all the choices make it hard to decide what to put on the table tonight. To lead you through this maze, we have identified key foods for health and energy, which can be kept in your store cupboard and used as the basis of everyday tasty eating.

Although the typical 21st-century life is clearly quite different from traditional subsistence routines, the evidence suggests the human body still functions in much the same way. But the nature of our foods and eating opportunities, as well as the extra demands we place on our bodies, mean that a traditional way of eating is neither possible nor appropriate any longer.

Smart nutrition

Our knowledge of nutrition, and especially our understanding of what may or may not promote better body function, has increased enormously in the last 20 years. With this new knowledge has come an element of confusion, as new discoveries override older ones. In today's busy life, who has time to sift through all the latest information to find out the most important factors in healthy eating? This is where *Smart Food* comes to the rescue – working out the key factors for healthier eating, then showing how these can be slotted into our lifestyle without sacrificing time or taste. Some of our ideas dispel entrenched food myths, some reinforce what our grandmothers may have told us and some reflect the latest nutritional discoveries.

Kitchen basics

Getting the store cupboard healthy is a two-step process. First, you need to identify what are the critical elements in food, and then you need to stock your store cupboard with convenient varieties of the foods which contain these elements. These become our 'smart food' basic ingredients.

Store cupboard ingredients

Beans, canned or dried (borlotti beans, butter beans cannellini beans, chickpeas, kidney beans, lentils, soy beans)
Fruit, canned (peaches, pears, rhubarb)
Fruit, dried (apricots, cranberries ('Craisins'), currants, raisins, sultanas)
Milk (skim condensed milk, skim evaporated milk)
New potatoes, canned
Noodles, dried
Nuts (almonds, brazils, pecans, pine nuts, pistachios, walnuts)
Pasta, dried

Rice (basmati, Doongara 'Clever Rice', Uncle Ben's 'Express Rice')
Rolled oats
Salmon, canned
Sardines, canned

Refrigerator ingredients
Eggs, omega-enriched
Feta
Milk, low-fat
Ricotta
Yogurt, low-fat (plain and flavoured – honey, vanilla, etc.)

Freezer ingredients
Filo pastry
Frozen vegetables (beans, corn, peas, spinach)
Frozen berries

Fresh ingredients
Garlic
Green onions
Herbs
Lemons
Onions
Red (Spanish) onions
Salad ingredients – mixed leaves and tomatoes
Seasonal fruit and vegetables

fuel it right

- *Do you eat some type of bread, cereal, muffin, fruit or yogurt within an hour of getting up?*
- *Does your main meal always contain some form of potato, pasta, noodle, rice, bread or other grain product?*
- *Do you often work or play for more than 3 hours without having something to eat?*

Answer no to any of these and you are short changing yourself on fuel.

Every machine requires specific fuel, and your body is no different. Unfortunately, it is not immediately obvious what is the best fuel: although your body prefers to operate on mainly one kind of fuel, carbohydrate, you need some of all types of food fuel regularly. Excess fuel – whatever the source – will be converted to fat.

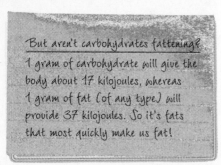

But aren't carbohydrates fattening?
1 gram of carbohydrate will give the body about 17 kilojoules, whereas 1 gram of fat (of any type) will provide 37 kilojoules. So it's fats that most quickly make us fat!

Despite the claims of trendy diet books, it is the carbohydrate in food that the body needs constantly, no matter what time of the day or what other foods you are eating. This basic fuel comes from the classic staples, so the message is to bring back bread, potatoes, pasta, rice and fruit throughout the day. Modern technology has created a new appreciation of how these foods work, leading to two important new tips for fuelling right.

Small and frequent

Because the body cannot handle too much of even its preferred food at once, the most effective way of giving your body the fuel it needs is grazing – small and frequent meals or snacks. An excess of even the 'good' carbohydrates will still be turned into fat. What's more, the human body does not have adequate storage capacity to keep the machine going for hours on end.

Modern-day lifestyles seem to have missed this point, forcing many of us to work, study or play for long stretches of time without stopping to refuel. We are able to do this because the body has in-built compensation mechanisms that come into operation when it senses any short-term deficit of carbohydrates. Unfortunately, even short-term starvation causes metabolic changes that put a strain on the system. Immediately you feel you have less energy, and in the long term there is greater wear and tear on the body.

Recent research from the UK confirms what we really know if we stop to think about it. When the gap between eating occasions is long, you become hungrier and so it becomes a lot harder to control your food intake. Simply not eating creates overeating.

Carbo it slow

Even among carbohydrates, not everything is equal. During digestion some carbohydrate foods percolate more slowly into our system than others. The technical term for the rate that a carbohydrate releases energy (in the form of glucose) into your body is its glycemic index, or GI. The index is simply a comparison of the rate glucose from the food enters the blood stream compared with a similar amount of straight glucose.

If a food is quickly digested, it moves straight into the blood system, producing a significant and rapid increase in blood-sugar levels. These types of foods have a high GI. Foods with a *low* GI move more *slowly* into the body, thereby supplying a more sustaining energy flow than a higher GI food. This special attribute of particular carbohydrate foods can be used to our advantage: a steadier energy supply increases feelings of fullness, so increased use of low GI foods can help to control appetite. And, in the long term, eating patterns with a low GI overall are thought to moderate some of the risks of heart disease and diabetes. This slower process is generally easier for the body to handle.

Simply fuelling regularly with low GI foods is a great basis for healthy eating.

The table below lists 'slow' foods – those that fall into the low GI range – and we have used combinations of foods in our recipes to ensure that the finished dishes have the lowest GI possible.

SLOW FOODS: low GI foods

Breads	wholegrain breads
	all Burgen-type breads
	pumpernickel
	pita breads (wholemeal and white)
	all fruit loaf breads
Biscuits	9-grain Vitawheat
	shredded wheatmeal
Cereals	rolled oats
	untoasted muesli
	oat-based cereals
	All Bran (and variants)
	Mini-Wheats
	Special K
	Vita Brits

Rice	basmati
	Doongara 'Clever Rice'
	Uncle Ben's 'Express Rice'

Pasta	all types and shapes

Other grains	barley
	cracked wheat (burghul)

Legumes	beans (baked, borlotti, cannellini, chickpeas, kidney, soy etc.)
	lentils (all types)

Vegetables	new potatoes
	sweet potatoes

Fruits	all fruits are good carbohydrates, but the farther from the equator a fruit is naturally grown, the slower it will release its glucose into the body – apples are one of the 'slowest' fruits

Dairy	all dairy foods are slow, but reduced-fat varieties have the winning combination of a low GI, high levels of calcium and low levels of fat

MEDIUM FOODS: medium GI foods

Grains	couscous
	polenta

Sources: *The G.I. Factor*, J. Brand-Miller, K. Foster-Powell, S. Colagiuri and A. Leeds (Hodder, 1998);
www.glycemicindex.com

fat – we need it

- *Do you think all fats are bad?*
- *Do you use only one kind of oil, such as olive oil?*
- *Is your fat intake less than 20 grams per day?*

Answer yes to any of these and you should read on . . .

Despite popular myth, fat is not a dirty word – it is just as vital for complete body function as the nutrients with a better public image, such as vitamins and minerals.

Certainly some individuals are eating too much fat, but everyone needs a certain amount of fat to function properly. This is because there are particular fats (so-called essential fats) which cannot be manufactured within the body, and so must be consumed as part of our food.

Interestingly, if the body does not gain adequate fat for normal daily functioning, this has the effect of signalling to the body to conserve or switch-off extra energy-burning processes. So a very low-fat diet can result in the body actually trying to save fat – quite the opposite of what may be desired!

Furthermore, it has recently been discovered that the fats known as 'omega-3 fats' are critical in the balancing of our inflammatory system. These fats are found in almost every part of our body, acting as controllers for an amazing number of vital processes. Because of the universal role of these fats, experts suggest that most people would benefit by increasing their intake of foods containing them. Research suggests that individuals with higher intakes have decreased risk of heart attacks, less fatty accumulation in blood vessels and fewer inflammatory reactions, which trigger uncomfortable conditions such as arthritis and asthma. We also know that omega-3 fats are crucial for early brain development.

Wherever possible, we have included foods high in omega-3 fats in our recipes, as well as using appropriate amounts of added fats.

Foods high in omega-3 fats include:

Fish	blue-eyed cod
	deep-sea perch
	gemfish
	mackerel, fresh or canned
	salmon, fresh or canned
	sardines, fresh or canned
	tailor
	tuna, fresh or canned
Seafood	calamari
	crayfish
	oysters, fresh or canned
	prawns
	scallops
Eggs	omega-enriched eggs
Oils	canola oil
	walnut oil
Vegetables	broccoli
	brussels sprouts
	cabbage
	Chinese greens
	green beans
	green capsicum
	leeks

	silver beet
	spinach
	watercress

Nuts and seeds	linseeds
	pecans
	walnuts

Legumes and pulses	all canned beans
	baked beans
	canned and frozen peas
	soy products (tempeh, tofu, etc.)

Fat fighting

- **Quantity.** Our recipes use a wide range of oils, but the quantities have been adjusted to ensure good taste while keeping within the limits recommended for best health.
- **Variety.** Different fats have different properties and benefits, and it is important to select the right type of fat for each recipe to ensure the best result. Using a variety of oils helps to ensure that you get the full range of fat-soluble vitamins and other essential nutrients.
- **'Invisible' fat.** Some food ingredients have a naturally high fat content, such as nuts. This can create a dilemma, but the modern mantra of 'all things in moderation' still holds good. Nuts are very useful foods: not only do they contain essential fats, but also some protective anti-oxidants (see below). Similarly, many people have become unnecessarily concerned about eating pork and red meat because of misapprehensions about the type and amount of fat they contain; if meat is free of visible fat (white fat), the 'invisible' fat levels will not be excessive.

The body needs protein foods daily, but too much of even

the leanest meat or fish provides surplus protein, which again is likely to be stored in the body as fat, so you should aim to have small servings (around 125 g) of all protein foods. A lean 125 g pork steak or beef fillet is ideal, but a 350 g piece of fish is excessive. Our recipes are devised to help you learn good portion sizes.

The new protectors

- *Do you consume at least 2 pieces of fruit (fresh, canned or dried) and about 2½ cups of salad and/or vegetables daily?*
- *Do you eat a few nuts on a daily basis?*
- *Do you use dairy (or equivalent) products daily?*

Answer no to any of these and you're not eating enough of the protective foods your body needs.

The oxygen paradox

Every cell of your body requires oxygen to live, but this vital oxygen is also slowly killing you! When oxygen lies unused in the body, it reacts with and 'activates' otherwise harmless substances, turning them into new, dangerous configurations. These are now known to act as triggers for many of the destructive ageing and disease processes, including most cancers and cardiovascular degeneration.

If left unchecked, this oxidation process would cause the body to break down very quickly. Fortunately, many protective mechanisms operate to neutralise the excess oxygen, rendering it harmless. The main substances that fuel these protective processes are anti-oxidants, which are found in a wide range of foods. Some of the better-known anti-oxidants are beta carotene (which is made into vitamin A in the liver), vitamin C, vitamin E, selenium and zinc, but the protective roles of many others are still being discovered.

Identifying the protective foods

- **Colour power.** Gran had the right idea, insisting that there were at least three colours of vegetables or salad on the dinner plate. Different-coloured fruits and vegetables contain different anti-oxidants, so the greater number of different-coloured foods you use, the more likely it is that your meal will contain a broad range of protective ingredients. Fill your plate with the more intensely coloured foods – such as beetroot, cranberries, blueberries, liquorice and red cabbage – as well as the green, red and orange foods.

- **Nut power.** Fascinating research has shown that nuts and some seeds are particularly powerful in protecting against certain types of oxidation. However, lots of nuts do not guarantee more protection; overdoing it by eating your way through the whole bag while watching TV merely gives you an excessive fat intake that soon outweighs any anti-oxidant benefits. Instead, get into the habit of adding a small amount (about a tablespoon) of nuts to cereals, salads, etc.

- **Bean power.** Pulses and legumes, as these foods are properly called, have many health advantages. Apart from providing an appropriate amount of protein in a normal helping, they contain small amounts of the vital omega-3 fats and are good sources of the types of fibre that help 'good bugs' to flourish in the small intestine. They also contain many of the more recently identified anti-oxidant substances. Beans are often perceived to be difficult foods to use – needing prolonged soaking and cooking. However, many varieties are available ready-to-use in cans or vacuum packs; these are ideal for long-term storage and make a very quick and convenient 'smart food'.

For longer, healthier life and to protect the body against the extra stresses of living in the 21st century – with all the heat, smog, cigarette smoke, chemicals and other destructive substances we are exposed to – the more protective anti-oxidants we consume, the better. While it is possible to gain some anti-oxidants from supplements, this is very limiting; there are many forms and variations of each naturally occurring anti-oxidant in foods that are not yet fully understood and cannot be captured in bottles.

So, more than ever before, it is vital to eat a variety of foods to ensure that the body has an adequate supply of anti-oxidants. Important protective foods include all fruits and vegetables, pulses, wholegrain cereals, nuts, and oils that contain vitamin E, such as canola.

calcium for all

Not only is calcium vital to build and maintain the strength of bones but it is now known that a good calcium intake helps the body to regulate blood pressure and stabilise other functions.

We have also incorporated calcium-rich foods in our recipes. Many foods contain calcium, but an excellent source is yogurt. In addition to containing lots of calcium in a form that is easily absorbed by the body, it is also a 'slow' carbohydrate, making it a fantastic snack.

In fact, the best thing about 'smart food' is that when you start to eat smart foods for one thing, you'll discover that you're actually eating smart for the whole body.

snacks appetisers & dips

Roast Capsicum and Tomato Relish

Makes about 2 cups

3 large red capsicums, deseeded and cut in half
1 tablespoon olive oil
1 × 400 g can whole tomatoes, drained
2 cloves garlic, finely chopped
1 teaspoon ground cumin
¼ teaspoon chilli paste
2 tablespoons lemon juice
salt and freshly ground black pepper
¼ cup freshly chopped flat-leaf parsley

Chargrill the capsicums, skin side up, under a very hot grill until the skin is black and blistered. Remove and place in a plastic bag to steam for 4 minutes, then peel off the skin and roughly chop the flesh.

In a large frying pan, heat the oil, then add the tomatoes, garlic and cumin. Cook for about 5–8 minutes until soft and pulpy. Remove and allow to cool before adding the capsicum, chilli paste and lemon juice. Finally, season with salt and pepper and stir in the chopped parsley.

This relish is delicious served on squares of toasted wholegrain bread, and can also be served with grilled fish or tossed through pasta.

Tsatziki

Makes about 2 cups

1 large telegraph cucumber
2 cloves garlic, crushed
2 tablespoons finely chopped fresh mint
1 tablespoon extra-virgin olive oil
1 cup plain low-fat yogurt

Cut the cucumber in half lengthways and scoop out the seeds. Finely chop the cucumber and drain in a colander. Mix the garlic, mint, oil and yogurt together and stir through the cucumber.

Chill until ready to serve.

This Greek dip is delicious served with grilled fish or chicken. You can also add it to sandwiches, or serve simply with toasted pita bread and vegetable crudities.

Spicy Sweet Potato and Tofu Dip

Makes about 2 cups

1 cup mashed, cooked sweet potato
2 teaspoons sweet chilli sauce
125 g silken tofu, drained
1 tablespoon lemon juice
1 tablespoon finely chopped chives

In a food processor, blend the sweet potato, chilli sauce, tofu and lemon juice together until smooth. Remove and stir in the chopped chives.

Served with toasted wholemeal pita bread and vegetable crudities.

Fresh Mango and Capsicum Salsa with Tuna

Serves 4–8

2 ripe mangoes, peeled and stones removed
1 small red capsicum, deseeded
2 tablespoons lime or lemon juice
1 tablespoon chopped chives
1 teaspoon sweet chilli sauce
6 tablespoons finely chopped fresh coriander
1 tablespoon mayonnaise
1 × 450 g can tuna, drained
salt and pepper
1 loaf Turkish bread, to serve

Cut the mango flesh and red capsicum into small chunks, then combine with the lime or lemon juice, chopped chives, sweet chilli sauce and coriander. Mix the mayonnaise and tuna together and season with salt and pepper.

Cut the Turkish bread through the middle, brush the cut sides with a little oil and grill until browned. Cut into sixteen small squares, spread each with a little tuna mayonnaise, top with a dollop of mango salsa and serve immediately.

This summery salsa works equally well with canned red salmon, sardines or mackerel.

Pecan and Lentil Paté

Serves 4–6

1 × 400 g can lentils
1 teaspoon ground turmeric
4 cloves garlic, crushed
pinch of salt
5 tablespoons lemon juice
300 ml vegetable stock
1 teaspoon hot curry powder
3 tablespoons miso
1 cup finely chopped pecan nuts

In a saucepan, heat the lentils, turmeric, garlic, salt, lemon juice and stock. Bring to the boil and simmer for about 5 minutes. Add the curry powder and miso, and cook for a further 10 minutes. Remove from the heat and allow to cool a little before blending the paté in a food processor. Stir through the chopped nuts, taste for seasoning and chill until ready to serve.

Serve with chopped fresh tomatoes, a mixed-leaf salad and wholemeal pita bread.

Miso is a great 'smart' ingredient for adding flavour to soups, casseroles and dips.

Roast Mushrooms with Pine Nuts

Serves 4–6

500 g large flat field mushrooms
juice of ½ lemon
2 tablespoons olive oil
2 cloves garlic, peeled and crushed
2 cups fresh wholemeal breadcrumbs
¼ teaspoon fresh thyme leaves
salt and freshly ground black pepper
2 tablespoons pine nuts, dry-roasted in a pan until golden

Preheat the oven to 200°C, and brush a baking dish with a little oil.

Wipe mushrooms with damp cloth, remove stems and chop finely. Dip the whole mushroom caps in the lemon juice and place them stem side up in the baking dish. In a frying pan, heat the oil and add the garlic, breadcrumbs, thyme and chopped mushroom stems. Sauté for 2–3 minutes, then season well with salt and pepper and stir in the pine nuts. Remove from the heat. Spoon the mixture into the mushroom caps and bake for 15–20 minutes.

Serve on a bed of mixed salad leaves, or on crusty Italian bread smeared with a little low-fat ricotta.

This mushroom dish makes a filling appetiser, and can also be served as an accompaniment to roast meats or grilled fish.

Chicken Empanadas

Makes about 18

1 tablespoon olive oil
1 small onion, finely chopped
1 teaspoon finely minced garlic
250 g finely minced raw chicken
1 cup ready-made tomato and vegetable pasta sauce
1 tablespoon pimento-stuffed olives, chopped
1 tablespoon raisins, roughly chopped
2 tablespoons finely chopped fresh coriander
salt and freshly ground black pepper
12 sheets filo pastry
a little milk for glazing the pastry

Preheat the oven to 180°C, and lightly grease a baking sheet.

In a saucepan, heat the olive oil, add the onion, garlic and chicken and cook for about 3–4 minutes, stirring constantly. Add the pasta sauce and cook until the liquid has reduced a little, then stir in the olives, raisins and coriander. Season with salt and pepper, remove from the heat and allow to cool completely.

Lay one sheet of filo on the bench and brush lightly with milk. Place another sheet on the top, then cut into three strips. Take a tablespoonful of the filling and place it on the end of one of the strips, then fold the sides in and roll up like a sausage. Continue filling and rolling until you have used up all the pastry and filling. Brush the tops of the empanadas with the milk and place on the baking sheet. Bake for 15–20 minutes until lightly browned. Remove and cool a little, before serving with fruit chutney or chilli sauce on the side.

Crab, Corn and Sweet Potato Cakes

Makes 8 potato cakes

500 g sweet potatoes, peeled and cut into chunks
1 tablespoon lime juice
1 green onion, finely chopped
2 × 170 g cans crab meat, drained
1 × 310 g can corn kernels, drained
freshly ground black pepper
1 omega-enriched egg, lightly beaten
½ cup polenta (cornmeal)

Boil the sweet potato until soft (about 15–20 minutes), leave to cool and then lightly mash with a fork. Stir in the lime juice, green onion, crab meat, corn kernels, pepper and beaten egg. Form into eight round patties and gently roll in the polenta. Chill until ready to cook.

Preheat the oven to 180°C and lightly grease a baking sheet. Place all the patties onto the baking sheet and bake for 15–20 minutes until crisp and heated through.

Serve with sweet chilli sauce and salad.

Omega-enriched eggs are produced by hens fed a particularly nourishing diet, which they obligingly convert into eggs with about six times the omega-3 content of regular eggs.

The biggest dieting myth is 'don't eat'. If you don't eat something every three hours, the body starts to build up extra appetites that are harder to control. So frequent, small meals and snacks are the way to go.

soups &
sandwiches

Lentil and Tomato Soup with Feta

Serves 4

2 teaspoons extra-virgin olive oil
1 large onion, finely chopped
4 large tomatoes, peeled, deseeded and roughly chopped
1 × 400 g can lentils
2 cups tomato juice
3 cups chicken or vegetable stock
½ teaspoon dried thyme
salt and freshly ground black pepper
40 g feta, crumbled
2 tablespoons freshly chopped flat-leaf parsley

In a saucepan, heat the oil and add the onion. Cook over a gentle heat until soft. Add the tomatoes, lentils, tomato juice, stock and thyme, then slowly bring to the boil. Cover and simmer for about 10 minutes. Season with salt and pepper.

Ladle into bowls and garnish with the feta and parsley.

Phytoestrogens, found in all pulses and beans and many fruits and vegetables, have a similar structure to estrogens and have a comparable role in the body. Among other things, they help circulation and cholesterol regulation, so a good intake is important for both men and women.

Mexican Bean Soup

Serves 4–6

1 tablespoon light olive oil
2 onions, finely chopped
3 cloves garlic, finely chopped
1 teaspoon ground cumin
1 teaspoon ground coriander
1 teaspoon chilli paste
1 × 400 g can red kidney beans
2 cups vegetable or chicken stock
1 × 400 g can diced tomatoes
1 small avocado, diced
2 tablespoons plain low-fat yogurt
1 cup corn chips

In a large saucepan, heat the oil and add the onion, garlic, cumin, coriander and chilli paste. Cook over a low heat until the onion is soft, then stir in the kidney beans, stock and tomatoes. Slowly bring to the boil, cover and simmer for about 20 minutes.

Serve topped with a little avocado and a dollop of yogurt, and garnished with a few corn chips.

Sweet Potato, Pumpkin and Corn Chowder

Serves 4–6

1 tablespoon canola oil
2 onions, peeled and finely chopped
500 g pumpkin, peeled and cut into small chunks
500 g sweet potatoes, peeled and cut into small chunks
3 cups vegetable or chicken stock
1 × 425 g can creamed corn
½ cup skim milk
2 tablespoons finely chopped chives
Worcestershire sauce, to serve

In a saucepan, heat the oil and add the onions, then cook over a gentle heat until soft. Add the pumpkin, sweet potatoes and stock and slowly bring to the boil. Simmer for 10–15 minutes, until the vegetables are just cooked. Add the creamed corn and milk, heat through for 5–10 minutes, then stir in the chopped chives.

Ladle into soup bowls and add a dash of Worcestershire sauce to each bowl.

Mushroom and Pearl Barley Soup

Serves 4–6

1 tablespoon olive oil
1 onion, finely chopped
2 cloves garlic, finely chopped
2 large celery sticks, finely chopped
500 g mushrooms, wiped clean and roughly chopped
¼ cup pearl barley
4 cups chicken or vegetable stock
1 tablespoon miso
salt and freshly ground black pepper
¼ cup finely chopped parsley

In a saucepan, heat the oil and add the onion, garlic, celery, mushrooms and barley. Cook over a low heat for 20 minutes, then pour in the stock and bring to the boil. Cover and simmer for 40 minutes, until the barley is tender and the soup has thickened. Stir in the miso and add salt and pepper to taste.

Ladle into soup bowls and garnish with parsley.

Kidney Bean, Corn and Spinach Soup

Serves 4–6

1 tablespoon olive oil
1 onion, finely chopped
2 cloves garlic, crushed
1 carrot, finely chopped
1 stick celery, finely chopped
1 × 310 g can corn kernels, drained
1 × 400 g can kidney beans, drained
3 cups vegetable or beef stock
250 g frozen spinach, defrosted and well-drained
2 tablespoons diced lean ham (optional)

In a large saucepan, heat the oil and gently cook the onion, garlic, carrot and celery for 4–5 minutes, stirring occasionally. Add the corn and kidney beans and pour in the stock. Bring to the boil, cover and simmer for 20 minutes. Stir in the spinach and cook for 5 more minutes, until heated through.

Serve in deep bowls, garnished with diced ham, if using.

Madras Pork Wraps
with Yogurt and Mint

Serves 4–8

1 tablespoon peanut oil
250 g lean minced pork
1 tablespoon Madras curry paste
1 red onion, finely chopped
salt and freshly ground black pepper
1 × 400 g can chickpeas or lentils, drained
2 tablespoons plain low-fat yogurt
1 tablespoon finely chopped fresh mint
4 slices Mountain Bread (cornmeal or wholemeal)
chilli sauce or fruit chutney, to serve

Heat the oil in a frying pan or wok over a medium heat,
add the pork and stir-fry for 2–3 minutes. Lower the heat
and add the curry paste and onion. Stir-fry for a further
2 minutes, then season to taste. Add the chickpeas or
lentils and cook for another 4–5 minutes, or until heated
through. Remove from the heat and stir in the yogurt and
mint.

Cut the Mountain Bread slices in half and spread a little
of the pork mixture at one end. Roll up and serve while
still warm, with some chilli sauce or fruit chutney on the
side.

Chickpea Omelette Rolls with Cucumber, Tomato and Yogurt Salad

Serves 4

1 × 400 g can chickpeas, rinsed and drained
½ teaspoon ground cumin
½ teaspoon ground coriander
1 cup flat-leaf parsley leaves
2 cloves garlic, crushed
1 teaspoon finely grated lemon zest
1 tablespoon lemon juice
1 tablespoon light olive oil
salt and freshly ground black pepper
8 omega-enriched eggs
½ cup skim milk
2 tablespoons tahini
4 wholemeal rolls

Salad
1 cup plain low-fat yogurt
1 small Lebanese cucumber, finely chopped
1 large ripe tomato, finely chopped
4 tablespoons finely chopped fresh mint
1 teaspoon sugar

Mash the chickpeas with a potato masher, just enough to crush them. Mix in the cumin and coriander, parsley, garlic, lemon zest and juice, the olive oil and salt and pepper.

Whisk together the eggs and milk in a mixing bowl. Heat a non-stick frying pan and spray a little oil over the bottom. Ladle about ½ cup of the egg mixture into the pan and cook over a medium heat until set underneath. Spoon over a quarter of the chickpea mixture and continue cooking until the top of the omelette is firm. Remove and keep warm while you cook the rest of the omelettes.

Combine the salad ingredients in a bowl and add seasoning to taste. Spread a little tahini onto each roll, slide in an omelette and top with some salad. Serve warm or at room temperature.

There are a greater number of bugs in the gut than there are cells in the body. To keep your 'good bugs' happy and your gut healthy, give them plenty of different types of fibre. And increase their numbers with yogurts that contain strains of Acidophilus bacteria and/or ones that stimulate the Bifido bacteria.

Cheesy Mushroom Burgers

Serves 4

1 tablespoon olive oil
1 onion, finely chopped
100 g flat field mushrooms, finely chopped
1 teaspoon mixed herbs
1 omega-enriched egg, lightly beaten
1 cup fresh wholegrain breadcrumbs
3 tablespoons grated tasty cheese
2 tablespoons finely grated parmesan cheese
2 teaspoons toasted sesame seeds
salt and freshly ground black pepper
4 pocket breads
4 lettuce leaves, shredded
2 tomatoes, finely sliced
1 small red onion, finely sliced

Cook the onion in the oil until soft. Add the mushrooms and herbs. Transfer to a bowl and stir in the egg, breadcrumbs, cheeses, sesame seeds and salt and pepper. Shape into four large patties, and chill until ready to cook.

Preheat the oven to 200°C, and lightly spray a baking tray with light olive oil. Bake the mushroom burgers for about 15 minutes until lightly brown and crisp on the outside.

Serve in pocket bread with the lettuce, tomato and onion.

Chicken-burgers on Wholegrain Rolls

Serves 4

Burgers
1 large clove garlic, finely chopped
2 green onions, finely chopped
500 g minced raw chicken
½ teaspoon black pepper
1 omega-enriched egg

Toppings
1 × 225 g can beetroot, drained
4 leaves of lettuce, shredded
1 carrot, finely grated
2 large tomatoes, thinly sliced

To serve
4 wholegrain rolls
2 tablespoons mayonnaise

Mix all the burger ingredients until well combined, then chill for 20 minutes. Prepare the toppings and spread a little mayonnaise onto each of the rolls.

Heat the grill or barbecue. Remove the chicken mixture from the refrigerator, and form into four patties. Grill for 6–8 minutes each side, or until the juices run clean when pierced with a skewer. (Alternatively, cook in a preheated 200°C oven for 15–20 minutes.)

Place a chicken-burger in each roll, add a selection of the prepared toppings and serve immediately.

Black Olive Cornbread

1 cup cornmeal
1 cup plain flour
1 tablespoon baking powder
¼ cup castor sugar
½ teaspoon chilli paste
1 omega-enriched egg, lightly beaten
¼ cup canola oil
1¾ cups buttermilk
2 tablespoons chopped chives
1 × 310 g can corn kernels, well drained
½ cup stoned and chopped kalamata olives

Preheat the oven to 180°C, and lightly oil a 28 cm × 18 cm baking tin. Mix the cornmeal, flour, baking powder and sugar together in a bowl.

In another bowl, thoroughly combine the chilli paste, egg, oil and buttermilk, then stir in the chives, corn and olives. Mix wet into dry ingredients, being careful not to over-mix. Pour the cornbread mixture into the prepared tin and bake for 30–35 minutes, or until lightly browned and cooked through.

Cornbread is great spread with ricotta, served with soup or to accompany roast vegetables and grilled meat.

salads

Grilled Marinated Tuna or Swordfish with Lentil Salad and Rocket

Serves 4

400 g tuna or swordfish, cut into 4 thick steaks
or
400 g canned tuna or sardines (do not marinate if using canned fish)
1 bunch rocket

Marinade
1 tablespoon finely grated orange zest
1 tablespoon balsamic vinegar
1 tablespoon extra-virgin olive oil
freshly ground black pepper

Salad
1 × 400 g can lentils, drained
2 tomatoes, roughly chopped
1 red onion, roughly chopped
250 g green beans, blanched for 2 minutes in boiling water,
    refreshed in cold water and roughly chopped
100 g new potatoes, cooked and sliced
or
½ × 310 g can new potatoes, drained and sliced

Dressing
4 tablespoons finely chopped parsley
2 tablespoons torn basil
1 clove garlic, finely chopped
2 teaspoons balsamic vinegar
1 tablespoon extra-virgin olive oil

In a metal or glass bowl, mix together all the marinade ingredients and add the fish, stirring to coat the pieces. Set aside for 30 minutes. Place all the salad ingredients in another bowl, then combine the dressing ingredients and stir through.

Heat a grill or barbecue and brush a little oil over the fish. Grill the fish for 3–4 minutes each side; the centre of the fish should still be pink. Cut the fish into chunks and toss through the salad.

Arrange the rocket on individual plates and spoon some of the fish salad over the top. Serve warm or cold.

Vinegar and citrus juices (lemon, lime, orange) magically slow down the rate of carbohydrate absorption from foods. So splashing some vinegar onto salads and vegetable dishes — for example, potatoes with an oil and vinegar dressing — turns them into slower foods.

Chargrilled Summer Vegetable Salad with White Beans and Herb Dressing

Serves 4

1 large eggplant, halved and cut into 1 cm thick slices
1 red, green or yellow capsicum, deseeded and cut into 8 pieces
1 bunch asparagus, stalks trimmed
1 red onion, sliced into thick rounds
1 × 400 g can cannellini beans, rinsed and drained

Dressing
1 tablespoon red wine vinegar
2 cloves garlic, finely chopped
1 tablespoon extra-virgin olive oil
salt and pepper
3 tablespoons chopped fresh herbs (mint, thyme, rosemary, oregano, basil)
2 tablespoons chopped fresh parsley
⅓ cup pitted black olives, roughly chopped

Mix together all the dressing ingredients in a bowl. Heat the grill or barbecue and cook the vegetables in batches, tossing them into the bowl of dressing as they are cooked. Mix in the beans, pile the salad onto a platter and serve with crusty bread.

Prosciutto and Kidney Bean Salad

Serves 4

olive oil spray
4 slices prosciutto, cut into strips
1 small red capsicum, deseeded and finely chopped
2 cloves garlic, finely chopped
½ cup ready-made tomato pasta sauce
1 tablespoon lime juice
1 × 400 g can kidney beans, rinsed and drained
2 tomatoes, roughly chopped
1 small red onion, finely chopped
1 avocado, peeled and finely chopped
salt and freshly ground black pepper
1 mignonette lettuce, washed and leaves separated

Heat a frying pan and lightly spray with olive oil. Cook the
prosciutto for 2–3 minutes. Add the capsicum and garlic
and cook for 1–2 minutes then pour in the pasta sauce and
lime juice. Stir in the beans and heat through. Remove and
allow to cool completely. Stir in the tomatoes, onion and
avocado, then season with salt and pepper.

Pile onto mignonette lettuce leaves and serve at room
temperature.

Barbecued Fish on Asian Cabbage Salad

Serves 4

4 fish steaks (swordfish, tuna, mahi mahi or barramundi)
½ Chinese cabbage, finely shredded
1 cup blanched snowpeas
1 × 200 g can baby sweetcorn, drained

Dressing
½ cup light soy sauce
1 teaspoon sugar
1 tablespoon finely grated ginger
¼ cup lime juice

Grill the fish until just cooked. Mix the cabbage, snowpeas and sweetcorn in a bowl, pour in the combined dressing ingredients and toss through.

Serve the grilled fish on top of the salad.

Tuna with Roast Sweet Potato and Spinach Salad

Serves 4

600 g sweet potatoes, washed and cut into small chunks
4 cloves garlic, peeled but left whole
1 tablespoon extra-virgin olive oil
juice and finely grated zest of 1 lemon
salt and freshly ground black pepper
1 bunch English spinach, washed and coarse stalks removed
1 × 450 g can tuna, drained

Preheat the oven to 180°C.

Place the sweet potato and garlic cloves onto a baking sheet and drizzle over the oil. Bake for 20–30 minutes until the sweet potato is cooked and lightly browned. Remove and allow to cool a little, then pour over the lemon juice and lemon zest and season with salt and pepper. Tear the spinach leaves into small pieces. Gently stir the drained tuna and roast sweet potato through the spinach just before serving.

Thai-style Chicken Salad in Lettuce Cups

Serves 4

250 g lean minced raw chicken
1 tablespoon fish sauce
1 tablespoon finely chopped lemongrass
1 small red onion, finely chopped
4 tablespoons chicken stock
2 small tomatoes, finely chopped
1 small mango, peeled and finely chopped
1 butter lettuce, washed and leaves separated

Dressing
1 green onion, finely chopped
1 tablespoon finely chopped fresh coriander
2 tablespoons finely chopped fresh mint
2 teaspoons lemon juice
1–2 teaspoons sweet chilli sauce, to taste

In a saucepan, cook the chicken with the fish sauce, lemongrass, onion and chicken stock for 10–15 minutes, breaking up the mince with a fork as it cooks. Remove from the heat and set aside to cool. Combine all the dressing ingredients in a large bowl. Add the tomato and mango, then the cooled chicken mixture, and stir to mix through.

Spoon the chicken salad onto the lettuce leaves and serve immediately.

Tempeh Salad with New Potatoes, Snowpeas and Walnuts

Serves 4–6

olive oil spray
1 × 610 g can baby potatoes, quartered
200 g snowpeas, trimmed
1 tablespoon sweet soy sauce (kecap manis)
1 tablespoon lemon juice
1 tablespoon olive oil
125 g tempeh, cut into small dice
1 tablespoon finely chopped walnuts
mixed salad leaves, to serve

Preheat the oven to 190°C.

Spray a non-stick frying pan with a little olive oil and pan-fry the potatoes until lightly browned. Transfer to a bowl and leave to cool. Blanch the snowpeas in boiling water for 2 minutes and refresh in cold water, then slice in half and add to the bowl. Mix the sweet soy, lemon juice and oil together and pour over the salad. Add the diced tempeh and walnuts and stir through. Serve piled on top of mixed salad leaves.

Try using spicy marinated tofu instead of tempeh for a totally different flavour.

Thai Beef Salad in Lettuce Cups

Serves 4–6

250 g lean minced beef
3 tablespoons water
1 tablespoon lemon juice
1 tablespoon fish sauce
1 large red onion, thinly sliced
1 tablespoon chopped green onions
4 tablespoons roughly chopped fresh mint
1 tablespoon finely chopped fresh coriander leaves and stems
2 teaspoons sweet chilli sauce
100 g fine rice noodles (vermicelli), rehydrated in hot water and drained
250 g bean sprouts, rinsed and drained
2 carrots, peeled and finely grated
a few mint leaves, for garnish

In a saucepan, cook the beef in the water for 2–3 minutes; the beef should still be a little pink. Transfer to a bowl, and stir in the lemon juice, fish sauce, onions, mint, coriander and sweet chilli sauce. Combine the rice noodles, bean sprouts and carrots and divide between individual serving plates. Spoon over the spicy beef and serve immediately, garnished with fresh mint leaves.

Fresh herbs add that special flavour to a salad. Keep them in the fridge with their stems in water and their tops covered with a plastic bag.

Crab and Cabbage Salad with Soy Dressing

Serves 4–6

2 × 170 g cans white crab meat, drained
½ Chinese cabbage, thinly shredded
1 Lebanese cucumber, deseeded and thinly sliced
4 green onions, thinly sliced
250 g bean sprouts, rinsed and drained

Dressing
1 tablespoon canola oil
2 teaspoons peanut butter
4 tablespoons white vinegar
1 teaspoon castor sugar
2 teaspoons soy sauce
1 clove garlic, finely chopped
½ teaspoon chilli paste
1 tablespoon coriander leaves
1 tablespoon crushed roasted peanuts

Mix all the dressing ingredients together. In a large bowl, combine the crab and vegetables. Pour over the dressing and gently stir through. Leave to marinate for at least 15 minutes before serving, garnished with coriander leaves and peanuts.

Greek Lentil Salad
with Red Capsicums,
Red Onions and Feta

Serves 4–6

1 × 400 g can lentils, drained
1 red capsicum, deseeded and finely chopped
1 red onion, finely chopped
18 kalamata olives, stones removed
100 g feta, crumbled
3 tablespoons finely chopped fresh mint

Dressing
1 tablespoon walnut oil
2 tablespoons red wine vinegar
pinch of ground cumin
salt and freshly ground black pepper

Mix together all the dressing ingredients and pour over the lentils. Toss in the capsicum and onion, then scatter the olives, feta and chopped mint over the top.

Serve with crusty bread and green salad.

Asian Chicken Salad

Serves 4

½ barbecued chicken *or* 300 g smoked chicken breast
1 bunch rocket
250 g bean sprouts, rinsed and drained
200 g cellophane (mung bean) noodles, rehydrated as per packet instructions
1 large avocado, cut into small dice
1 small papaya, cut into small dice

Dressing
6 tablespoons lime or lemon juice
finely grated zest of 1 lime
2 tablespoons canola oil
2 teaspoons honey
2 tablespoons chopped chives
1 clove garlic, crushed
1 teaspoon chilli paste

Remove the skin and bones from the chicken and cut the meat into strips. Combine all the dressing ingredients in a bowl.

To serve, place a mixture of rocket, bean sprouts and cellophane noodles onto a serving platter, mound the chicken on top, and add a spoonful of avocado and papaya. Pour over the dressing and serve immediately.

Prawn and Rice Salad
with Fresh Mango

Serves 4

12 cooked prawns, peeled, deveined and roughly chopped
2 cups cooked basmati rice or Doongara 'Clever Rice'
1 large firm mango, peeled and diced
¼ cup finely chopped red onion
2 tablespoons lemon juice
1 tablespoon olive oil
salt and freshly ground black pepper
mint or coriander leaves, for garnish
4 lemon wedges

In a large bowl, combine the prawn meat, rice, mango, onion, lemon juice and oil. Season to taste with salt and pepper.

Mound onto individual plates, garnish with mint or coriander leaves and a lemon wedge on the side.

pasta & pizza

Easy Spring Vegetable Pasta

Serves 4

1 tablespoon extra-virgin olive oil
3 cloves garlic, finely chopped
1 cup fresh wholegrain breadcrumbs
200 g dried spinach or corn spaghetti or fettucini
1 cup frozen peas
1 cup frozen green beans
1 tablespoon finely grated parmesan

Heat the oil in a frying pan and cook the garlic for 1 minute over a low heat. Stir in the breadcrumbs and gently fry for 2–3 minutes until lightly browned and toasted. Cook the pasta in plenty of boiling salted water until just done. Remove and keep warm. Using the pasta water, cook the frozen vegetables. Drain and stir through the pasta.

Just before serving, stir through the garlic breadcrumbs and parmesan.

Many frozen vegetables are snap-frozen minutes after picking, and so are often nutritionally superior to 'fresh', which can be several days away from picking when purchased.

Fishy Pasta Bake
with Prosciutto

Serves 4

350 g dried pasta bows or shells
4 slices of prosciutto, cut into strips
1½ cups ready-made tomato pasta sauce
finely grated zest of 1 lemon
500 g firm fish fillets, cut into bite-sized pieces
4 tablespoons fish stock or white wine
3 tablespoons freshly chopped basil
2 tablespoons finely grated parmesan

Cook the pasta in a large pot of boiling water until tender, remove and drain.

Meanwhile, cook the prosciutto in a saucepan over a gentle heat for 2–3 minutes. Stir in the pasta sauce and bring to the boil. Add the lemon zest, fish and stock or wine and cook for 3–4 minutes, until the fish is just cooked. Stir in the chopped basil. Remove and stir through the cooked pasta.

Preheat the grill. Spoon the pasta into a shallow heatproof dish and sprinkle over the parmesan. Place under the hot grill until the cheese has melted and is lightly browned.

Serve with a mixed-leaf salad or steamed green vegetables.

Pasta with Fresh Herbs, Lemon and Roast Vegetables

Serves 4

1 sweet potato, washed and cut into small chunks
1 red capsicum, deseeded and cut into small pieces
1 eggplant, cut into small chunks
1 red onion, cut into small pieces
6 cloves garlic, peeled but left whole
2 tablespoons extra-virgin olive oil
1 × 225 g can whole beetroot, drained and cut into small chunks
freshly ground black pepper
250 g flat dried pasta (tagliatelle, fettucini)

Sauce
1 teaspoon finely grated lemon zest
4 tablespoons silken tofu, drained, or plain low-fat yogurt
1 tablespoon chopped nuts (walnuts, pecans or pine nuts)
½ cup freshly chopped mixed herbs (parsley, basil, chives and coriander)

Preheat the oven to 180°C.

Prepare the vegetables and place in a baking dish. Drizzle over the olive oil and bake for 20–30 minutes until they are tender. Remove, stir in the beetroot chunks, grind over some pepper and return to the oven for 5 minutes.

To make the sauce, place all the ingredients in a food processor and blend until smooth. Cook the pasta until just done. Stir the roast vegetables through the pasta, then serve in individual bowls with a spoonful of sauce over the top.

Rainbow Pasta Bake

Serves 4

250 g pasta spirals or macaroni
2 cups ready-made tomato pasta sauce
1 tablespoon olive oil
1 onion, finely chopped
1 clove garlic, crushed
1 small green capsicum, deseeded and cut into small chunks
1 small red capsicum, deseeded and cut into small chunks
1 cup frozen corn kernels
100 g low-fat ricotta
2 omega-enriched eggs, lightly beaten
salt and pepper
50 g grated cheddar cheese
2 tablespoons grated parmesan

Preheat the oven to 180°C, and lightly grease a large
rectangular baking dish (approximately 30 cm × 20 cm).

Cook the pasta in plenty of boiling water until tender
but still firm. Drain, stir in the pasta sauce and set aside.
Put the oil in a frying pan and cook the onion, garlic and
capsicums for 3–4 minutes over a gentle heat until soft.
Remove and stir through the pasta, together with the corn
kernels. Beat the ricotta and eggs, and season with salt and
pepper. Spoon the pasta into the baking dish, spread over
the ricotta mixture and sprinkle the top with parmesan and
cheddar cheeses. Bake for 30–35 minutes until the cheese
has browned and the pasta is heated through.

Easy Lasagne

Serves 6

1 tablespoon olive oil

1 onion, finely chopped

3 cloves garlic, finely chopped

1 large zucchini, cut into small cubes

1 medium eggplant, cut into small cubes

2 × 400 g cans diced tomatoes

1 × 400 g can soy beans, rinsed and drained

¼ cup kalamata olives, stones removed and roughly chopped

½ teaspoon Italian dried herbs

salt and freshly ground black pepper

1 cup low-fat ricotta

¼ cup plain low-fat yogurt

1 omega-enriched egg

6 large sheets oven-ready 'instant' lasagne

4 tablespoons grated parmesan

Preheat the oven to 200°C, and lightly grease a rectangular baking dish (approximately 35 cm × 22 cm).

In a saucepan, heat the oil and cook the onions and garlic over a low heat until soft. Add the zucchini and eggplant and cook, stirring occasionally, for 4–6 minutes. Pour in the tomatoes, soy beans, olives and herbs. Bring to the boil and then simmer for 6–8 minutes. Remove from the heat and season with salt and pepper. Beat together the ricotta, yogurt and egg until smooth and creamy.

Lay two sheets of pasta in the baking dish. Spoon over half the tomato sauce, cover with another two sheets of pasta, and then spoon in the rest of the sauce. Top with the last two pasta sheets, smooth the ricotta mixture over the top and sprinkle over the parmesan. Bake for 20–25 minutes until lightly browned, then turn the heat down to 180°C and cook for a further 10 minutes. Remove from the oven and let stand for 5 minutes before serving.

The ricotta and yogurt topping makes this a great high-calcium meal.

Lentil and Vegetable Pasta with Crispy Prosciutto

Serves 4–6

300 g small dried pasta shells
¼ cup plain low-fat yogurt
6 slices prosciutto, grilled until crispy

Sauce
1 tablespoon olive oil
1 large onion, finely chopped
1 fennel bulb, finely chopped
3 sticks celery, finely chopped
1 teaspoon ground cumin
1 × 400 g can diced tomatoes
2 × 400 g cans lentils
2 tablespoons tomato paste
½ teaspoon chilli sauce
salt and freshly ground black pepper

First, make the sauce. Heat the oil in a saucepan and cook the onion, fennel, celery and cumin for 3–4 minutes until soft. Stir in the tomatoes and lentils. Bring to the boil and simmer, covered, for 20 minutes or until the lentils are soft. Stir in the tomato paste, chilli sauce and season with salt and pepper. Cook the pasta in plenty of boiling water until tender. Drain and stir in a little of the sauce.

Serve in deep pasta bowls with the sauce poured over the top, spoon a little yogurt on the top and garnish with the crispy prosciutto.

Sicilian Silver Beet Pizza

Serves 4

2 tablespoons currants
2 tablespoons golden raisins
olive oil spray
1 red onion, cut into thin wedges
1 bunch silver beet, washed and coarse stalks removed
1 tablespoon balsamic vinegar
pinch of ground nutmeg
freshly ground black pepper
1 frozen pizza base
½ cup grated mozzarella
1 tablespoon grated parmesan
¼ cup coarsely chopped almonds

Preheat the oven to 200°C.

Soak the currants and raisins in hot water for 10 minutes. Lightly spray a non-stick frying pan with olive oil, and cook the onion over a high heat for 3–4 minutes until lightly browned. Shred the silver beet, add to the pan and cook until wilted. Drain the currants and raisins and stir them into the pan, then add the balsamic vinegar, nutmeg and pepper and cook for 1 minute. Remove from the heat and leave to cool a little.

Spread the silver beet mixture over the pizza base and sprinkle over the mozzarella, parmesan and almonds. Bake for 15–20 minutes, or until the pizza base is cooked through. Cut into slices and serve.

Small, shiny, dark-brown linseeds are one of the best omega-3 booster foods. A spoonful of the ground seeds (often called 'linseed meal') can be sprinkled over morning cereal, salads or fruit salad, or blended into a smoothie. They should always be stored in the fridge to prevent rancidity.

rice
& couscous

Risotto Primavera

Serves 4

1 cup vegetable stock
1 cup white wine
1 tablespoon olive oil
1 leek, washed and finely chopped
1 cup Doongara 'Clever Rice' or risotto rice
1 cup frozen peas
salt and freshly ground black pepper
2 tablespoons freshly chopped parsley
¼ cup crumbled low-fat feta
1 tablespoon finely grated parmesan

Combine the stock and wine in a saucepan, bring to the boil and then turn down to a gentle simmer. In another saucepan, heat the oil and cook the leek over a gentle heat until soft. Pour in the rice and cook for 2–3 minutes, stirring all the time. Add about ½ cup of hot stock to the rice and cook, stirring constantly, until the liquid has been absorbed. Continue until all the stock has been used and the rice is tender (about 15–20 minutes), then stir in the peas and cook for about 4 minutes. Season well with salt and pepper and stir in the chopped parsley.

To serve, spoon into bowls and sprinkle over a little feta and parmesan.

Risotto Cakes

Shape any leftover risotto into patties and place on a lightly greased baking sheet. Bake in a preheated 190°C oven for 6–8 minutes or fry in a lightly greased non-stick frying pan for 5 minutes each side, until lightly browned. Serve with a mixed-leaf salad.

Prawn and Spring Vegetable Risotto

Serves 4

1 litre (4 cups) fish stock
pinch of saffron threads
1 tablespoon canola oil
1 large onion, finely chopped
1 clove garlic, finely chopped
1½ cups Doongara 'Clever Rice' or risotto rice
½ cup frozen peas
½ cup frozen green beans
1 bunch fresh asparagus, cut into small pieces
250 g raw prawns, peeled and deveined
or
175 g frozen, uncooked prawn meat
salt and freshly ground black pepper
2 tablespoons finely chopped flat-leaf parsley

Heat the fish stock in a saucepan, add the saffron and keep at a gentle simmer until ready to add to the risotto. In a separate saucepan, heat the oil and cook the onion and garlic until lightly browned and soft. Add the rice and stir for 2–3 minutes. Add the hot stock a little at a time, stirring constantly until all is absorbed before adding more. Continue until all the stock has been used and the rice is tender (about 15–20 minutes), then add the vegetables and stir until heated through. Finally, stir in the prawns and cook for 3–4 minutes until just cooked.

Season well with salt and pepper and serve immediately, garnished with chopped parsley.

Rice-stuffed Tomatoes with Olives and Basil

Serves 4

8 medium-sized, firm tomatoes
salt and freshly ground black pepper
1 tablespoon extra-virgin olive oil
3 cloves garlic, finely chopped
1½ cups cooked Doongara 'Clever Rice' or risotto rice
2 tablespoons vegetable stock
2 teaspoons lemon juice
4 anchovy fillets, soaked in milk for 10 minutes then finely chopped
200 g pimento-stuffed green olives, roughly chopped
¼ cup finely chopped fresh basil
salt and freshly ground black pepper
mixed salad leaves

Cut the tops off the tomatoes and reserve. Carefully scoop out the seeds and discard the flesh. Season the tomato cups with salt and pepper, then turn them upside down to drain on kitchen paper.

Heat the oil in a small saucepan and cook the garlic over a low heat until soft. Remove from the heat and stir into the cooked rice, together with the stock, lemon juice, anchovies, olives, basil and salt and pepper to taste. Stuff the tomatoes with the rice mixture and replace the tops.

Serve immediately, with a handful of mixed salad leaves.

Stuffed Cabbage Leaves with Rice and Almonds

Serves 4

12 large Chinese cabbage leaves or 8 medium-sized green cabbage leaves
1 cup basmati rice or Doongara 'Clever Rice', well rinsed
¼ cup roughly chopped toasted almonds
1 tablespoon sultanas
½ × 400 g can diced tomatoes
1 small red onion, finely chopped
1 teaspoon freshly chopped mint, or ½ teaspoon dried mint
¼ teaspoon finely grated lemon zest
salt and freshly ground black pepper
⅔ cup vegetable stock
4 lemon wedges

Preheat the oven to 180°C.

Bring a large pot of water to the boil and blanch the cabbage leaves for 2–3 minutes until limp. Remove and drain, then trim each leaf to a rectangle – about 10 cm × 5 cm. In a mixing bowl, combine the rice, almonds, sultanas, tomatoes, onion, mint and lemon zest. Add salt and pepper to taste. Place a heaped tablespoon of rice mixture on each cabbage leaf and roll up to make a neat parcel. Secure with a toothpick. Place the stuffed cabbage leaves in a casserole dish and pour over the stock. Cover and bake for 30 minutes.

Serve with mashed sweet potatoes and a mixed-leaf salad, with lemon wedges on the side.

Lemon Pilau Rice

Serves 4

1 tablespoon canola oil
1 onion, finely diced
1 teaspoon finely grated ginger
1½ cups basmati rice
3 cups chicken stock
juice and finely grated zest of 1 lemon
1 tablespoon chopped parsley
salt and freshly ground black pepper

Heat the oil in a saucepan and gently cook the onion and ginger for 2–3 minutes until soft. Stir in the rice and cook for 1 minute. Add the stock and cook for 10–15 minutes, covered, until almost all the stock has been absorbed. Stir in the lemon juice and zest and parsley. Season with salt and pepper before serving.

Pilau rice can be served alongside grilled fish or chicken; it is also delicious on its own with a spoonful of tomato chutney.

Aromatic Coconut Rice

Serves 4

1¼ cups water or vegetable stock
1 cup basmati rice or Doongara 'Clever Rice'
½ cup light coconut milk
½ teaspoon ground turmeric
¼ teaspoon salt
¼ teaspoon ground cardamom
1 stick cinnamon
½ teaspoon chilli powder

Bring the water or stock to the boil and stir in the rice, coconut milk and all the spices. Cover the saucepan, bring back to the boil and then turn the heat to low and simmer for 15 minutes. Remove the cinnamon stick and fluff the rice with a fork. Serve immediately.

Serve this flavourful rice with grilled fish, chicken, or steamed vegetables.

Yellow and Green Rice

Serves 4

1 tablespoon canola oil
1 small onion, finely chopped
4 whole cardamom pods
2 sticks cinnamon
1 teaspoon finely grated ginger
½ teaspoon ground turmeric
1 cup basmati rice
1½ cups vegetable stock
250 g packet frozen spinach, defrosted and drained

Heat the oil in a heavy-based saucepan and cook the onion
with the spices for 2–3 minutes. Stir in the rice and sauté
for 1–2 minutes, then pour in the stock and bring to the
boil. Cover tightly, turn the heat to very low and cook for
15–20 minutes. Stir in the spinach and let stand for
8 minutes before serving.

Among other goodies, greens contain
folate. Not only is this important
for pregnant women to consume, but
good intakes also appear to give
protection from heart disease.

Curried Rice, Beans and Vegetable Pilaff

Serves 2–4

⅓ cup mango chutney
2½ cups vegetable stock
1 tablespoon olive oil
1 medium onion, finely chopped
2 cloves garlic, finely chopped
1 cup basmati rice or Doongara 'Clever Rice'
1 tablespoon curry powder
1 × 400 g can soy beans, rinsed and drained
1 small sweet potato, peeled and cut into small chunks
½ cup 'Craisins' (dried cranberries)
1 × 250 g packet frozen chopped spinach, defrosted and drained
plain low-fat yogurt, for garnish

Blend the mango chutney and stock together and set aside. Heat the oil in a non-stick frying pan and cook the onions and garlic over a low heat until soft. Add the rice and curry powder and stir-fry for 2–3 minutes. Add the beans, sweet potato, 'Craisins' and stock mixture, and stir well. Bring to the boil, then cover the pan and reduce the heat to a simmer. Cook for about 20 minutes until rice and vegetables are tender, and the liquid has been absorbed. Remove from the heat, stir in the spinach, cover and let stand for 10 minutes.

Serve in shallow bowls, garnished with a dollop of yogurt.

Spicy Rice with Grilled Vegetables

Serves 4

1 tablespoon olive oil
1 onion, sliced into rings
2 cloves garlic, chopped
pinch of chilli powder
1 teaspoon mixed spice
1 cup basmati rice or Doongara 'Clever Rice'
2 cups vegetable stock
10 dried apricots, chopped
1 yellow or green capsicum, deseeded and cut into strips
1 red capsicum, deseeded and cut into strips
1 large eggplant, thinly sliced lengthways
2 tablespoons roasted pecan nuts
salt and freshly ground black pepper

In a large saucepan, heat the oil and fry the onion and garlic until soft. Mix in the spices, cook for a minute and then add in the rice. Stir until all the grains are coated with oil. Pour in the stock and bring to the boil. Stir in the apricots, reduce to a simmer, cover the pan and cook for about 25 minutes, until the liquid is absorbed and the rice is tender.

Meanwhile, preheat the grill or barbecue. Grill the capsicums and eggplant until browned on both sides. Fold the vegetables and nuts into the rice and add salt and pepper to taste. Serve immediately.

Moroccan Chicken with 'Craisin' Couscous Salad

Serves 4

½ teaspoon ground cumin
½ teaspoon ground coriander
pinch of salt
freshly ground black pepper
4 small chicken breast fillets (approximately 500 g in total)
juice of 1 lemon
1 tablespoon extra-virgin olive oil

Couscous salad
2 cups chicken stock
2 cups quick-cook couscous
pinch of salt
juice of 2 lemons
1 tablespoon extra-virgin olive oil
1 small clove garlic, finely chopped
½ cup finely chopped fresh mint
2 cups finely chopped parsley
1 small red capsicum, deseeded and finely chopped
½ cup 'Craisins' (dried cranberries), soaked in hot water for 10 minutes

To make the couscous salad, bring the chicken stock to the boil in a pan. Pour in the couscous, cover the pan and remove from the heat. Leave to stand for 2 minutes, stir with a fork and let stand for another 3 minutes. Place the couscous in a bowl, stir in the salt, lemon juice, olive oil and garlic. Leave until cool, then stir through the rest of the ingredients.

Preheat the oven to 200°C. Combine the cumin, coriander, salt and pepper, and rub over the chicken fillets. Mix together the lemon juice and oil, brush over the chicken, then place on a baking sheet and roast for 10 minutes. Allow the chicken to cool a little before cutting into strips and arranging on top of the couscous salad on a serving platter.

Use a bought barbecued chicken if time runs out — just remove the skin and then cut the meat into thin strips.

Dried cranberries (marketed as 'Craisins') are a delicious snack, and seem to be particularly high in protective phytochemicals — especially one that may help with prostate function.

Easy Couscous and Chickpeas

Serves 4

1 cup water
1 cup quick-cook couscous
½ cup Moroccan Tagine sauce (page 124), or vegetable or chicken stock
1 × 400 g can chickpeas, drained
1 teaspoon chilli paste

Bring the water to the boil in a pan. Pour in the couscous, cover the pan and remove from the heat. Leave to stand for 2 minutes, stir with a fork and let stand for another 3 minutes. Put the Tagine sauce or stock into a deep frying pan, add the chickpeas and heat through. Stir in the couscous and chilli paste. Serve immediately.

This makes a great accompaniment to Moroccan Tagine (page 124) or can be served as a light lunch with Tsatziki (page 17).

Spicy Lamb and Couscous Salad

Serves 4

400 g lamb fillets
1 tablespoon Madras curry powder

Salad
1 cup water
1 cup quick-cook couscous
½ cup diced cucumber
¼ cup diced green onions
¼ cup finely chopped fresh mint
juice of 1 lemon
1 tablespoon olive oil
2 tablespoons mango chutney
salt and white pepper
fresh mint, for garnish

Rub the lamb fillets with the curry powder and cook on a lightly oiled barbecue or under a hot grill, turning once, for 3 minutes each side. Remove and set aside to cool.

To make the salad, bring the water to the boil in a pan. Pour in the couscous, cover the pan and remove from the heat. Leave to stand for 2 minutes, stir with a fork and let stand for another 3 minutes. Transfer the couscous to a bowl, then stir in the cucumber, green onions and mint. Mix the lemon juice, oil and mango chutney together and pour over the couscous. Season well with salt and pepper.

Thinly slice the cooled lamb fillets and toss through the salad. Serve in bowls, garnished with sprigs of fresh mint.

vegetarian mains

Zucchini and Semi-dried Tomato Slice

Serves 4–6

1 tablespoon wheatgerm
500 g zucchini, grated and drained
1 large onion, finely chopped
¼ cup finely grated parmesan
1 cup unbleached self-raising flour
4 omega-enriched eggs, lightly beaten
¾ cup diced semi-dried tomatoes
salt and freshly ground black pepper

Preheat the oven to 180°C, lightly grease a 25-cm square tin and sprinkle the wheatgerm over the bottom.

In a large bowl, thoroughly mix all the ingredients together, leaving aside one-quarter of the semi-dried tomatoes. Pour the zucchini mixture into the prepared tin, sprinkle the top with the reserved semi-dried tomatoes, and bake until set, about 30 minutes.

Cool a little in the tin before removing and cutting into squares. Serve hot, warm or cold with salad.

Wheatgerm adds extra
B vitamins — use as here or
sprinkle a tablespoonful over a
bowl of cereal.

Sweet Potato and Feta Frittata

Serves 4–8

350 g sweet potato, cut into small chunks and steamed or roasted
200 g feta, cut into small chunks
8 omega-enriched eggs
2 tablespoons ricotta
pinch of ground nutmeg
salt and freshly ground black pepper
6 green onions, finely chopped
2 tablespoons finely grated parmesan

Preheat the oven to 180°C, and line a 28 cm × 18 cm tin with non-stick baking paper.

Scatter the cooked sweet potato and feta into the baking tin. Beat the eggs, ricotta and nutmeg together, season well with salt and pepper, then stir in the onions. Pour the egg mixture over the vegetables, sprinkle over the parmesan and bake for 35–40 minutes, or until the eggs are set and the top is browned.

Remove from the tin, cut into squares and serve warm or cold.

This is great for using up leftover roast sweet potatoes.

Vegetable Tikka

Serves 4

8 metal or wooden skewers
100 g sweet potato, peeled and cut into chunks
4 tablespoons plain low-fat yogurt
3 tablespoons tikka curry paste
1 small red onion, cut into quarters
2 small eggplants, cut into 4-cm cubes
3 small zucchini, cut into 4-cm slices
1 red capsicum, deseeded and cut into chunks

If using wooden skewers, soak them in water for 10 minutes (this prevents them burning). Parboil the sweet potato for 4 minutes, drain and run under the cold tap to cool. Mix the yogurt and tikka paste together and then stir through the vegetables. Leave to marinate for about 30 minutes. Preheat the grill or barbecue, thread the vegetables onto the skewers and grill for 6–8 minutes, turning once, until the vegetables have softened and are lightly browned.

Remove and serve on top of boiled basmati rice, with fruit chutney and lemon wedges on the side.

Winter Vegetable and Tempeh Casserole

Serves 4

1 tablespoon canola oil
1 large onion, finely chopped
2 cloves garlic, finely chopped
200 g mushrooms, thinly sliced
300 ml vegetable stock
1 large sweet potato, peeled and cut into cubes
1 carrot, peeled and cut into cubes
2 parsnips, peeled and cut into cubes
1 cup frozen peas
400 g tempeh, cut into large cubes
¼ cup miso
¼ cup tahini
¼ cup peanut butter
2 teaspoons light soy sauce
1 tablespoon cider vinegar

Heat the oil in a large saucepan and cook the onion and garlic over a low heat until translucent. Add the mushrooms and sauté for 5 minutes. Pour in the stock and bring to the boil, then add the rest of the vegetables and simmer for 15 minutes. Add the tempeh and cook for a further 5 minutes. Ladle about one cup of hot broth into a bowl and blend it with the miso, tahini and peanut butter, soy sauce and vinegar. Pour back into the saucepan and heat through.

Serve in a deep bowl, spooned over boiled Doongara 'Clever Rice' or basmati rice.

Chilli Chickpeas with a Couscous Crust

Serves 4

1 tablespoon olive oil
1 teaspoon ground hot paprika
1 small onion, finely chopped
1½ cups ready-made tomato and vegetable pasta sauce
¾ cup vegetable stock
1 × 400 g can chickpeas, drained
salt and freshly ground black pepper
1 cup water
1 cup quick-cook couscous
2 tablespoons finely chopped parsley
1 tablespoon light olive oil

Heat the oil in a saucepan and add the paprika and onion. Cook for 3–4 minutes until the onion is lightly browned. Add the pasta sauce and stock, bring to the boil and simmer for about 20 minutes. Stir in the chickpeas, add salt and pepper to taste, and cook for a further 5 minutes.

Preheat the oven to 190°C. To make the couscous crust, bring the water to the boil in a pan. Pour in the couscous, cover the pan and remove from the heat. Leave to stand for 2 minutes, stir with a fork and let stand for another 3 minutes. Stir in the parsley and olive oil. Spoon the chickpeas into a baking dish, spoon the couscous over the top and bake for 30 minutes.

Cashew Nut Curry

Serves 4

3/4 cup raw cashew nuts
1/2 cup light coconut milk
1 cup vegetable stock
1 large onion, finely chopped
2 teaspoons green curry paste
1 stick cinnamon
2 strips lemon peel or 1 stalk lemongrass, roughly chopped
1 cup fresh or frozen green beans
1/2 cup frozen peas
1 cup fresh or frozen broccoli florets

Soak the cashew nuts in water for 30 minutes. Meanwhile, place the coconut milk, stock, onion, curry paste, cinnamon and lemon peel or lemongrass in a saucepan and simmer, uncovered, for 10 minutes. Drain the cashews, add to the curry and simmer for a further 15 minutes. Finally, add the beans, peas and broccoli and cook for a further 6–8 minutes, or until the vegetables are just cooked.

Serve with boiled basmati rice or Doongara 'Clever Rice'.

Nuts are full of nutrients, but it is little and often that wins the day. Recent research suggests that nutty eaters have fewer fatal illnesses; a tablespoon of nuts daily (about 15 g) is recommended.

Italian Vegetable Gateau

Serves 4

4 cups vegetable stock
1 cup polenta (cornmeal)
½ cup ready-made tomato pasta sauce
1 zucchini, thinly sliced lengthways
1 small eggplant, cut in half and thinly sliced lengthways
1 red capsicum, deseeded and thinly sliced
olive oil spray
½ cup low-fat ricotta
1 tablespoon finely grated parmesan
2 tablespoons shredded fresh basil leaves, for garnish
mixed salad leaves, to serve

Preheat the oven to 190°C.

Place the stock in a saucepan and bring to the boil. Slowly pour in the polenta, stirring constantly. Bring back to the boil and simmer for about 20 minutes, stirring occasionally. Pour into a flan tin (about 20 cm diameter) that has been rinsed with cold water, and press the polenta down to make a base. Spread the pasta sauce over the top, then arrange the sliced zucchini, eggplant and capsicum over the top, lightly spraying them with oil. Spread over the ricotta, sprinkle with parmesan and bake for 30 minutes until the vegetables are soft and the cheeses are lightly browned.

Garnish the gateau with basil, then cut into slices and serve with a mixed-leaf salad.

Cracked Wheat Pilaff with Pumpkin and Cashew Nuts

Serves 4

1 tablespoon olive oil

1 cinnamon stick

1 medium onion, finely chopped

225 g butternut pumpkin, peeled and cut into small chunks

⅓ cup coarse cracked wheat (burghul)

¾ cup vegetable stock

2 tablespoons chopped roasted cashew nuts

¼ cup crumbled feta

In a saucepan, heat the oil and gently fry the cinnamon stick and onion over a low heat for 2–3 minutes. Stir in the pumpkin and cracked wheat and cook, stirring constantly, for 4–5 minutes. Add the stock and bring to the boil, stirring constantly. Cover the pan, turn the heat to low and simmer for about 30 minutes. Turn off the heat, lift the lid and sprinkle over the cashew nuts. Place a clean tea towel over the top of the pan and replace the lid. Leave to stand for 15 minutes, then stir through the feta just before serving.

Indian Vegetable Pancakes

Serves 4

100 g chickpea flour (besan)
½ teaspoon baking powder
¼ teaspoon ground turmeric
1 teaspoon ground cumin
2 omega-enriched eggs
½ cup low-fat milk
¼ cup water
1 tablespoon finely grated ginger
2 tablespoons freshly chopped coriander
2 green onions, finely chopped
1 small carrot, grated (approximately 3 tablespoons)
1 medium zucchini, grated (approximately 3 tablespoons)
1 teaspoon chilli paste
olive oil spray

In a food processor, blend the flour, baking powder and spices, then mix in the eggs, milk and water. Transfer the pancake batter to a bowl and stir in the rest of the ingredients. Set aside until ready to cook.

Lightly spray a non-stick frying pan with olive oil and spoon tablespoonfuls of the mixture into the pan. Cook each pancake until the underside is browned, then flip over to brown the other side. Remove and keep warm until all the pancakes are done.

Serve with Tsatziki (page 17) and fruit chutney, or Roast Capsicum and Tomato Relish (page 16).

Mexican Corn Pudding

Serves 4–6

1 × 420 g can corn kernels
2 omega-enriched eggs, lightly beaten
2 cups (500 ml) buttermilk
1 × 400 g can diced tomatoes
1 small onion, finely chopped
½ green capsicum, deseeded and finely chopped
½ red capsicum, deseeded and finely chopped
⅔ cup kalamata olives, stoned and chopped
½ teaspoon chilli paste
1 cup yellow cornmeal
2 tablespoons olive oil
mixed salad leaves, to serve

Preheat the oven to 175°C, and lightly grease a 1.5 litre casserole dish.

In a mixing bowl, combine all the ingredients except the olive oil and salad leaves until well combined. Pour into the casserole dish, drizzle the oil over the top and bake for 35–45 minutes until firm and lightly browned on the top.

Let stand for 10 minutes, before serving with a mixed-leaf salad.

Cannellini Bean and Eggplant Gratin

Serves 4

1 large eggplant, peeled and cut lengthways into very thin slices
1 tablespoon olive oil
2 medium onions, finely chopped
2 cloves garlic, finely chopped
1 × 400 g can cannellini beans, drained
¼ cup finely chopped parsley
1 cup canned diced tomatoes
salt and freshly ground black pepper
½ cup fresh wholegrain breadcrumbs
2 tablespoons finely grated parmesan
mixed salad leaves, to serve

Preheat the oven to 180°C, and lightly grease a baking dish.

Place the eggplant slices, in a single layer, on a baking sheet lined with non-stick baking paper and bake until tender – about 10 minutes. Meanwhile, heat the oil in a frying pan and cook the onions and garlic over a gentle heat until soft, then remove from the heat and stir in the cannellini beans and parsley.

Line the sides and bottom of a gratin dish with eggplant and spoon over half the bean mixture, then half the tomatoes, seasoning the layers with salt and pepper. Cover with the rest of the eggplant slices, followed by the other half of the bean mixture and the tomatoes. Mix the breadcrumbs and parmesan together and sprinkle on top, then bake for 30–40 minutes until lightly browned.

Serve with a mixed-leaf salad.

Tofu and Sweet Potato Cakes

Serves 4

1 medium-sized sweet potato, peeled and cut into small cubes
1 tablespoon olive oil
1½ teaspoons Madras curry powder
1 small onion, finely chopped
1 clove garlic, finely grated
1 tablespoon tomato paste
400 g firm tofu, drained
½ cup fresh wholegrain breadcrumbs
salt and freshly ground black pepper

Steam the sweet potato until tender – about 10–15 minutes – and mash. Heat the oil in a non-stick frying pan and gently cook the curry powder, onion and garlic together for 2–3 minutes. Remove and mix into the sweet potatoes with the tomato paste. Squeeze as much moisture as possible out of the tofu and mash into the sweet potato mixture. Stir in the breadcrumbs and season well with salt and pepper. Form into four patties and refrigerate until ready to cook.

Preheat the oven to 220°C, and lightly grease a baking sheet. Place the sweet potato cakes on the baking sheet and bake for 15–20 minutes until lightly browned.

Serve with boiled rice and mango chutney.

Tofu made with calcium sulphate (sometimes listed as 509) is high in calcium, as well as being a good source of protein and phytoestrogens.

Mushroom, Spinach and Tofu Strudel

Serves 4

1 tablespoon olive oil
1 onion, finely chopped
1 clove garlic, finely chopped
500 g button mushrooms, roughly chopped
1 × 250 g packet frozen spinach, defrosted
1 cup silken tofu, drained and mashed with a fork
½ cup low-fat ricotta
½ cup fresh wholegrain breadcrumbs
1 omega-enriched egg, lightly beaten
salt and freshly ground pepper
5 sheets filo pastry
milk for glazing pastry

Preheat the oven to 190°C, and lightly grease a baking sheet.

Heat the oil in a non-stick frying pan and cook the onion and garlic over a low heat until soft. Add the mushrooms and cook for 4–5 minutes. Squeeze excess moisture out of the spinach and add to the pan. Cook for 2–3 minutes, then transfer the mixture to a bowl and leave to cool for about 20 minutes before stirring in the tofu, ricotta, breadcrumbs and egg. Season well with salt and pepper. Lay the sheets of filo pastry on the prepared baking sheet, brushing a little milk between the layers. Spoon the filling down the long side nearest to you, leaving a 10 cm border all round. Fold the short sides in and carefully roll up the strudel, ending with the seam side down. Bake for 30–40 minutes until crisp and browned.

Serve with steamed green vegetables or a mixed-leaf salad.

Potato, Carrot and Feta Pancake Stack with Tomatoes

Serves 4

2 large potatoes, peeled and grated
1 large carrot, peeled and grated
1 small onion, peeled and grated
pinch of salt
2 omega-enriched eggs
2 teaspoons dried thyme
100 g feta, crumbled
¼ cup plain flour
½ teaspoon lemon pepper seasoning
1 cup canned diced tomatoes
olive oil spray
mixed salad leaves and lemon wedges, for garnish

Mix the potato, carrot and onion together with the salt.
Place in a colander and leave to drain for 15–20 minutes.
In a bowl, lightly beat the eggs and stir in the thyme, feta,
flour and lemon pepper seasoning. Fold in the drained
vegetables. Gently heat the diced tomatoes in a saucepan.
While the tomatoes are heating, cook the pancakes. Spray
a little light olive oil into a non-stick frying pan. Heat the
pan until hot and then add 2 tablespoonfuls of batter
per pancake to the pan, flattening with a spatula as the
pancakes cook. Cook for 3–4 minutes each side, until
golden brown. Keep warm until all the pancakes are done
(you should have about eight).

Serve with some of the tomatoes sandwiched between two
pancakes. Garnish with salad leaves and lemon wedges.

Lentil and Vegetable Moussaka

Serves 4

olive oil spray
1 medium-sized eggplant, cut into thin rounds
1 medium-sized sweet potato, peeled and cut into thin rounds
1 tablespoon olive oil
1 large onion, finely chopped
1 large red capsicum, deseeded and finely chopped
1 large clove garlic, finely chopped
4 tablespoons red wine or vegetable stock
2 tablespoons tomato paste
½ teaspoon ground allspice
¼ teaspoon ground cinnamon
1 × 400 g can lentils, drained
salt and freshly ground black pepper

Topping
3 omega-enriched eggs
6 tablespoons plain low-fat yogurt
3 tablespoons finely grated parmesan
freshly ground nutmeg

Preheat the oven to 180°C, lightly grease a 35 cm × 22 cm baking dish.

Heat a chargrill pan or barbecue, spray the slices of eggplant and sweet potato with olive oil and then grill: the sweet potato will need about 3–4 minutes each side, the eggplant 2–3 minutes. Remove and set aside. Heat the oil in a non-stick frying pan and cook the onion, capsicum and garlic for 3–4 minutes until soft. Stir in the wine or stock, tomato paste and spices, cook for 2–3 minutes, then stir in the lentils and season with salt and pepper. Combine all the topping ingredients in a bowl and mix well.

Lay a third of the eggplant and sweet potato slices in the prepared baking dish, then cover with half the lentil mixture. Make another layer of sweet potato and eggplant, covering them with the rest of the lentil mixture. Top with the remaining sweet potato and eggplant slices, spread over the topping and bake for 30 minutes until lightly browned.

Apart from the great taste, a glass of red wine a day can help circulation, hence the association with heart health — just don't overdo it!

Twice-baked Sweet Potatoes

Serves 4

4 sweet potatoes (of similar size)
1 red onion, thinly sliced
olive oil spray
¾ cup low-fat ricotta
1 tablespoon plain low-fat yogurt
¼ teaspoon dried sage
½ teaspoon salt
¼ teaspoon freshly ground black pepper
¼ cup coarsely chopped pecan nuts
mixed salad leaves, to serve

Preheat the oven to 200°C.

Wash the potatoes well and prick the skins, then place in a baking dish with the onion and spray with a little olive oil. Bake for about 45 minutes or until tender when pierced with a fork. Remove from the oven and allow to cool a little before cutting the top off each potato, lengthways. Carefully scoop out the flesh with a spoon or melon baller, leaving the skins intact. Mash the flesh with the ricotta, yogurt, sage and salt and pepper, then stir in the baked onion. Spoon back into the potato shells and sprinkle over the chopped pecans. Turn the oven down to 160°C, put the potatoes back in the baking dish and return to the oven for 20 minutes.

Serve with a mixed-leaf salad.

fish & seafood

Steamed Fish with Rice Noodles and Lime and Sweet Chilli Sauce

Serves 4

1 tablespoon roughly chopped coriander leaves
1 tablespoon finely chopped garlic chives
2 cups cooked rice vermicelli noodles
4 × 125 g firm fish fillets (ling, snapper, salmon or ocean trout)

Sauce
½ cup light soy sauce
1 teaspoon finely grated lime zest
2 tablespoons lime juice
1 tablespoon sweet chilli sauce
2 tablespoons water

Preheat the oven to 180°C.

Mix all the sauce ingredients together in a bowl. Lay out four large sheets of non-stick baking paper – approximately 30 cm × 15 cm. Stir the herbs into the noodles, then divide the mixture into four equal portions. Place one portion on each sheet of baking paper, then arrange a fish fillet on top, cutting in half if necessary. Draw up the sides of the paper to make a parcel, folding in the sides. Spoon a little sauce into each parcel and then seal the top by folding over the join two or three times.

Place the parcels on a baking sheet and bake in the oven for 6–8 minutes, until the fish is cooked through. Serve immediately.

Spicy Pilau Rice with Snapper Fillets

Serves 4

1 tablespoon olive oil
1 onion, finely diced
1 teaspoon finely grated ginger
½ teaspoon ground allspice
1 teaspoon ground turmeric
salt and freshly ground black pepper
1½ cups basmati rice
3 cups vegetable or fish stock
2 cups defrosted frozen mixed vegetables (beans, peas and carrots)
300 g snapper or ling fillets, cut into chunks
1 tablespoon finely chopped parsley
2 teaspoons lemon juice
2 tablespoons blanched roasted almonds, chopped

Preheat the oven to 180°C.

Heat the oil in a saucepan and gently fry the onion, ginger and spices for 2–3 minutes. Add the rice to the pan and stir to coat with the spices. Pour in the stock and slowly bring to the boil, then cover and simmer for 10–12 minutes until nearly all the stock has been absorbed.

Spoon the rice into an ovenproof dish and stir in the vegetables, fish, parsley and lemon juice. Cover with foil and bake for 10 minutes, until the fish and vegetables are cooked through. Remove from the oven and serve garnished with chopped almonds.

Steamed Ling Fillets with Red Capsicum Sauce and Mashed Cannellini Beans

Serves 4

4 large outer leaves iceberg lettuce
4 × 150 g ling (or any other firm fish) fillets
finely grated zest of 1 lemon
salt and freshly ground black pepper
1 × 400 g can cannellini beans, drained
1 teaspoon extra-virgin olive oil

Sauce
2 red capsicums, cut in half and seeds removed
2 cloves garlic, crushed
1 teaspoon ground cumin
1 teaspoon white wine vinegar
1 cup ready-made tomato pasta sauce

To make the sauce, grill the capsicums until the skins have blistered and blackened, then place in a plastic bag for 10 minutes (the steam helps loosen the skin). Remove from the bag and peel off the skin. In a food processor, blend the capsicums with the garlic, cumin, vinegar and pasta sauce. Transfer the sauce to a pan and gently heat through.

Blanch the lettuce leaves in boiling water until limp. Remove and refresh under cold water, then pat dry with kitchen paper. Place a fish fillet in the middle of each lettuce leaf, and sprinkle with lemon zest and salt and pepper. Fold the lettuce leaf around the fish to form four neat parcels, then steam for 8–10 minutes, depending on the thickness of the fish. While the fish parcels are steaming, heat the beans through in a saucepan, then mash with a potato masher, adding the olive oil.

Remove the fish parcels from the steamer and serve with the mashed beans and red capsicum sauce.

Canned, cooked pulses (chickpeas, lentils or beans) are convenient and the nutritional value is just the same, so don't worry if you have no time for the prolonged soaking and cooking required for the dried version.

Spicy Fish and Sweet Potato Pies

Serves 4

1 large sweet potato, peeled and cut into small chunks
1 tablespoon canola oil
1 onion, finely chopped
1 teaspoon mild curry powder
500 g firm fish fillets (ling, barramundi, snapper or silver perch),
    cut into small chunks
4 tablespoons plain low-fat yogurt
1 tablespoon finely chopped chives
8 sheets filo pastry
1 omega-enriched egg

Preheat the oven to 200°C, and lightly grease a baking sheet.

To make the filling, boil the sweet potato until just tender (10–15 minutes). Heat the oil in a pan and lightly fry the onion with the curry powder for 3–4 minutes. Remove and cool before stirring in the sweet potato, fish, yogurt and chives.

Lay out two sheets of filo pastry, spoon a quarter of the fish mixture into the centre, and fold the pastry over to make a triangular parcel. Repeat until you have four parcels. Lightly beat the egg with a tablespoon of cold water, brush over the pies, then slide them onto the baking sheet. Bake for about 20 minutes, until puffed up and lightly browned.

Serve hot, accompanied by a mixed-leaf salad, and perhaps some tomatoes oven-roasted with a little olive oil.

Prawn and Green Onion Fritters

Serves 4–6

1 tablespoon canola oil
8 green onions, finely chopped
1 teaspoon Thai green curry paste
3 tablespoons finely chopped parsley
250 g fresh raw prawns, peeled, deveined and finely chopped
or
175 g frozen raw prawn meat, defrosted and chopped
1 carrot, peeled and finely grated
¾ cup plain flour
½ cup chickpea flour (besan)
½ teaspoon baking powder
1½ cups ice-cold water
olive oil spray

Heat the oil in a frying pan and cook the onions and curry paste for 2–3 minutes. Remove and combine with the parsley, prawn meat and carrot. Sift the flours together with the baking powder, then stir in the water to make a thick creamy batter. Stir through the prawn mixture and set aside for 30 minutes.

To cook the fritters, spray a non-stick frying pan with oil and ladle about 2 tablespoons of the batter mix into the pan. Cook for 3–4 minutes each side. Remove and keep warm until all the fritters are cooked. Serve with Cucumber, Tomato and Yogurt Salad (page 32).

Seared Tuna with Caperberry Dressing

Serves 4

4 thick tuna steaks (each weighing about 150 g and about 3 cm thick)
olive oil

Dressing
2 teaspoons finely grated lemon zest
2 tablespoons caperberries
4 tablespoons chopped chives
4 tablespoons coriander leaves, finely chopped
2 tablespoons extra-virgin olive oil
1 tablespoon balsamic vinegar

To serve
mixed salad leaves
4 ripe tomatoes, peeled, deseeded and diced
crusty wholegrain bread

Brush a little olive oil over the tuna. Heat a chargrill pan or barbecue until very hot, and cook the tuna steaks for about 2 minutes each side; the tuna should still be a little rare inside. Remove and leave to rest for a few minutes. In a non-reactive bowl (glass or plastic), mix together all the dressing ingredients. Cut the tuna into chunks and toss through the dressing.

Place a handful of salad leaves on each plate, top with a quarter of the tuna and garnish with diced tomato. Serve with crusty wholegrain bread.

This tuna dish is also delicious served on top of pasta, or with cannellini beans.

Chinese Broccoli Stir-fry with Tuna

Serves 4

1 tablespoon light olive oil
1 teaspoon sesame oil
4 green onions, sliced
2 cloves garlic, crushed
1 tablespoon finely grated ginger
2 bunches Chinese broccoli (gai lan), trimmed and washed
1 × 450 g can tuna, drained
1 tablespoon sesame seeds, briefly dry-roasted in a heavy-based pan

Sauce
1 tablespoon olive oil
1 tablespoon white wine vinegar
1 tablespoon sweet soy sauce

In a bowl, mix together all the sauce ingredients. Preheat a wok or frying pan over a high heat, then pour in the light olive oil and sesame oil. Add the green onions, garlic and ginger and stir-fry for 2–3 minutes. Toss in the Chinese broccoli and cook until wilted. Add the tuna, pour in the dressing and toss well. Remove to a serving bowl and sprinkle over the sesame seeds.

Serve with boiled rice or rice noodles.

Salmon Pies with Cheese and Corn

Serves 4

1 tablespoon canola oil
2 cloves garlic, crushed
4 green onions, finely chopped
1 × 240 g can salmon
2–3 tablespoons dry white wine
1 large cooked potato, peeled and roughly chopped
½ cup frozen corn kernels
2 tablespoons chopped chives
50 g tasty cheese, coarsely grated
salt and freshly ground black pepper
8 sheets filo pastry
milk for glazing the pastry

Preheat the oven to 200°C, and lightly grease a baking sheet.

Heat the oil in a frying pan and cook the garlic and green onions for 2–3 minutes, then transfer to a bowl. Add all the remaining ingredients except the filo pastry and the milk. Lay out two sheets of filo, spoon a quarter of the fish mixture into the centre, and fold the pastry over to make a triangular parcel. Repeat until you have four parcels, then brush the tops with a little milk. Slide the pies onto the baking sheet and cook for 10–15 minutes, or until lightly browned.

Serve immediately with a mixed-leaf salad.

Whole Baked Fish
with Pecan Couscous

Serves 4

½ cup fish stock or water
½ cup quick-cook couscous
1 tablespoon canola oil
1 onion, finely chopped
1 small carrot, grated
1 small zucchini, grated
⅓ cup finely chopped pecans
1 teaspoon finely grated lemon zest
salt and freshly ground black pepper
4 whole red-spot whiting, scaled and cleaned
lemon wedges, for garnish

Preheat the oven to 180°C, and lightly grease a baking dish big enough to hold the fish.

To make the couscous stuffing, bring the stock or water to the boil in a pan. Pour in the couscous, cover the pan and remove from the heat. Leave to stand for 2 minutes, stir with a fork and let stand for another 3 minutes.

Heat the oil in a frying pan over medium heat, add the onion and cook until soft. Transfer to a bowl, then add the couscous, carrot, zucchini, pecans, lemon zest and salt and pepper; mix well.

Pack the couscous stuffing firmly into the cavity of each fish, then arrange the fish in the prepared baking dish and cover with non-stick baking paper. Bake until fish is opaque and beginning to flake when tested, about 20 minutes.

Serve immediately, with lemon wedges and steamed green vegetables.

Other firm white fish, such as red mullet, baby snapper, silver perch, or baby barramundi, also work well with this interesting stuffing.

Stir-fried Squid with Potatoes

Serves 4

500 g fresh squid, cleaned (ask the fishmonger to do this for you)
or
375 g frozen squid tubes, defrosted
2 tablespoons olive oil
4 cloves garlic, finely sliced
1 × 600 g can baby new potatoes, drained
2 tablespoons finely chopped fresh mint
2 tablespoons finely chopped fresh coriander
2 teaspoons red wine vinegar

Cross-score the squid tubes and cut into strips; cut the tentacles into bite-size pieces. Heat the oil in a wok or large frying pan and cook the squid for 1–2 minutes until tender. Remove, add the garlic and potatoes and stir-fry for 2–3 minutes until browned. Return the squid and stir in the herbs and vinegar. Stir-fry for 1–2 minutes, then serve immediately.

This recipe also works well with uncooked peeled prawns, baby octopus, cuttlefish or chunks of firm fish such as ling or blue-eyed cod.

meat & poultry

Parcels of Chicken with Lime and Sweet Potatoes

Serves 4

4 small chicken breast fillets, cut in half
1 large sweet potato, peeled and thickly sliced
1 tablespoon canola oil
2 tablespoons pecan nuts, roughly chopped
1 lime, cut into 8 wedges

Marinade
juice and finely grated zest of 1 lime
3 cloves garlic, finely chopped
1 tablespoon finely grated ginger
½ teaspoon chilli paste
pinch of saffron threads (optional)
salt and freshly ground black pepper

Mix all the marinade ingredients in a bowl, pour over the prepared chicken fillets and leave to marinate for about half an hour. Meanwhile, steam the sweet potato for 5 minutes; it should still be firm.

Preheat the oven to 180°C, and cut four sheets of non-stick baking paper – approximately 20 cm × 15cm. Remove the chicken from the marinade and pat dry. Heat the oil in a frying pan and brown the chicken in batches. Place a quarter of the sweet potato on a sheet of the baking paper, top with two pieces of chicken, then draw together the sides of the paper to make a parcel, pouring in a little of the marinade before loosely sealing the top. Repeat with the other four parcels, place on a baking sheet and bake for 10 minutes, or until the chicken breast is cooked through.

Serve with Yellow and Green Rice (page 69), and garnish with chopped pecans and lime wedges.

Orange fruits and vegetables are the foods that give the best protection against certain cancers, where vitamins A and C in combination are required.

Chicken, Feta and Leek Strudels

Serves 4

1 tablespoon canola oil
1 large leek, washed, trimmed and finely chopped
1 red onion, finely chopped
2 cloves garlic, finely minced
400 g lean minced raw chicken
½ cup crumbled feta
1 teaspoon dried mint
1 teaspoon dried parsley
salt and freshly ground black pepper
4 sheets filo pastry
a little milk, for glazing pastry

Preheat the oven to 200°C, and line two baking sheets with non-stick baking paper.

Heat the oil in a saucepan, add the leek, onion and garlic, and cook for 3–4 minutes until soft. Add the chicken and cook for 3–4 minutes over a gentle heat until cooked through. Turn up the heat and cook for 3–4 minutes to evaporate some of the liquid. Remove from the heat and cool completely before stirring in the feta, herbs and salt and pepper.

Lay four sheets of filo on top of each other, brushing a little milk between the sheets. Cut down the centre. Place half the chicken filling at the short end of half the pastry, fold the sides in and roll up into a log. Repeat with the other half. Brush the two strudels with milk. Place on the prepared baking sheets and bake for 20–30 minutes, until lightly browned.

Remove and allow to cool a little before serving with a mixed-leaf salad.

Chicken Kebabs with Caribbean Sauce

Serves 4

1 cup nectarine juice
1 tablespoon lime or lemon juice
4 chicken breast fillets, cut into cubes
8 wooden skewers, soaked in warm water for 10 minutes
¼ cup chopped coriander leaves

Sauce
½ cup lemon or lime juice
½ cup tomato sauce (ketchup)
½ cup canned diced tomatoes
½ cup chopped green capsicum
½ cup frozen corn kernels, defrosted
2 teaspoons chilli paste
¼ cup brown sugar
2 tablespoons finely grated ginger
1 tablespoon rum (optional)

Mix the nectarine and lime juices together, pour over the chicken and leave to marinate for 30 minutes. Meanwhile, place all the sauce ingredients in a saucepan and stir over a gentle heat until well combined. Bring to the boil and simmer for 3 minutes. Remove and allow to cool a little.

Thread the marinated chicken onto the skewers, and preheat a chargrill pan or barbecue. Brush the chicken with a little oil, then cook for 3–4 minutes each side, until lightly browned and cooked through. Serve on Lemon Pilau Rice (page 67), with a spoonful of sauce drizzled over the top and garnished with chopped coriander.

Thai Chicken and Vegetable Curry

Serves 4

1 tablespoon canola oil
6 chicken thigh fillets, cut into chunks
1 yellow capsicum, deseeded and roughly chopped
1 red capsicum, deseeded and roughly chopped
2 small carrots, peeled and diagonally sliced
½ cup frozen green beans, defrosted
½ cup frozen peas
2 teaspoons Thai green curry paste
1 × 400 g can skim evaporated milk
2 tablespoons desiccated coconut
coriander leaves, for garnish

Heat the oil in a large frying pan or wok, and gently stir-fry
the chicken for 3 minutes. Add the capsicums and carrots
and stir-fry for 3 minutes more, then stir in the beans, peas,
curry paste, evaporated milk and desiccated coconut. Bring to
the boil and simmer gently for 2–3 minutes, until the
vegetables are just cooked.

Garnish with coriander leaves and serve with Lemon Pilau
Rice (page 67).

Roast Chicken Breasts with Macadamia and Waterchestnut Stuffing

Serves 4

4 medium-sized chicken breast fillets (approximately 150 g each)
¼ cup plain flour
1 omega-enriched egg, beaten with 1 tablespoon water
1 cup fresh wholemeal breadcrumbs (about 4 slices bread)

Stuffing
2 green onions, finely chopped
1 slice of prosciutto, finely chopped
1 teaspoon finely grated orange zest
¼ cup finely chopped macadamia nuts
½ cup roughly chopped canned waterchestnuts
2 tablespoons fresh multigrain breadcrumbs
salt and freshly ground black pepper
1 omega-enriched egg, lightly beaten

Mix all the stuffing ingredients together. Cut a large pocket in each of the chicken breasts, push in about 2 tablespoons of stuffing, and press the edges together to seal. Dust the chicken breasts with flour, then dip into the egg mixture and roll in the breadcrumbs. Chill for 20 minutes.

Preheat the oven to 220°C, and line a baking tray with non-stick baking paper. Place the chicken breasts on the tray and bake for 30–35 minutes, until cooked through. Serve with sweet potato mash and a green salad.

Spicy Summer Chicken

Serves 4

1 tablespoon canola oil

4 chicken breasts (or 8 chicken thighs), skin removed

1 onion, finely chopped

1 clove garlic, finely chopped

1 tablespoon Madras curry powder

1 tablespoon plain flour

2 cups chicken stock

½ cup light coconut milk

1 tablespoon redcurrant jelly

4 canned peach halves, thinly sliced

2 teaspoons lemon juice

1 teaspoon finely grated lemon zest

2 tablespoons chopped roasted cashew nuts, for garnish

Heat the oil in a large, heavy-based saucepan and lightly brown the chicken in batches over a medium heat, remove and set aside. In the same pan, fry the onion and garlic for 2–3 minutes, then add the curry powder and flour and cook, stirring constantly, for 1 minute. Pour in the stock a little at a time, stirring well, and bring to the boil. Simmer for 15 minutes, then return the chicken to the pan and cook for a further 35 minutes, or until the chicken is cooked through. Stir in the coconut milk, redcurrant jelly and peaches, and heat through for 2–3 minutes. Finally, stir in the lemon juice and lemon zest.

Serve with Lemon Pilau Rice (page 67) or plain boiled rice, and garnish with chopped cashew nuts.

Lemony Chicken with Raisins and Chickpeas

Serves 4

4 skinless chicken thigh fillets
or
1 whole chicken, jointed and skin removed
1 teaspoon finely chopped garlic
1 teaspoon ground turmeric
salt and freshly ground black pepper
1 large lemon, skin and pith removed and discarded,
    and flesh cut into very thin slices
¼ cup raisins
2 cups chicken stock
1 × 400 g can chickpeas
1 tablespoon lemon juice
1 tablespoon finely chopped parsley, for garnish

Preheat the oven to 175°C.

Arrange the chicken in a single layer in a large baking dish, and scatter over the garlic and turmeric. Season with salt and pepper, then spread the lemon slices and raisins on top. Pour over enough stock to cover the chicken. Bake for 30–35 minutes, or until the chicken is cooked through. Add the chickpeas and bake for a further 10 minutes. Remove the dish from the oven and pour the sauce into a saucepan. Add the lemon juice, bring to the boil and reduce by one third.

Serve the chicken on basmati rice or bow-shaped pasta, with the sauce spooned over the top, and garnished with parsley.

Pork Stuffed with Apple and Sage served with Root Vegetable Bake

Serves 4

1 onion, finely chopped
2 apples, peeled, cored and finely chopped
1 tablespoon canola oil
1 cup fresh multigrain breadcrumbs
1 teaspoon dried thyme
½ teaspoon dried sage
4 tablespoons finely chopped parsley
½ cup chopped pecan nuts
salt and freshly ground black pepper
¼ cup white wine or stock
4 lean pork schnitzels
olive oil spray

Vegetable bake
1 medium sweet potato, peeled and thinly sliced
2 waxy potatoes, peeled and thinly sliced
½ small butternut pumpkin, peeled and thinly sliced
1 cup vegetable or chicken stock
freshly ground black pepper

Preheat the oven to 200°C, and lightly grease a baking dish.

Layer the vegetables in the baking dish, press down and pour over the stock. Grind over some black pepper and bake for 20 minutes.

Meanwhile, prepare the stuffed pork. Lightly fry the onion and apples in the oil until soft and browned. Remove and stir in the breadcrumbs, dried and fresh herbs and chopped pecans, mixing well; season with salt and pepper. Moisten with a little wine or stock. Spread some of the stuffing onto each of the pork schnitzels, roll up and tie with string to make a parcel. In a non-stick frying pan sprayed lightly with oil, brown the pork parcels on all sides.

Sit the pork parcels on top of the vegetable bake, turn the oven down to 175°C and bake for a further 20 minutes. Remove the string from the pork and serve immediately with mustard or cranberry sauce on the side.

We know it takes more than an apple a day — but every little bit helps!

Roast Pork Chops with Mustard Vegetables

Serves 4

4 thick-cut lean pork chops, trimmed of visible fat
2 cloves garlic, finely chopped
1 large red onion, cut into wedges
2 large waxy potatoes, washed and cut into small wedges
1 sweet potato, washed and cut into thick chunks
1 large parsnip, peeled and cut into small wedges
1 fennel bulb, trimmed and cut into wedges
1 tablespoon canola oil
2 tablespoons Dijon mustard
1 tablespoon lemon juice
1 teaspoon finely grated lemon zest
½ cup chicken or vegetable stock
salt and freshly ground black pepper
finely chopped parsley, for garnish

Preheat the oven to 180°C.

Place the pork chops in a large baking dish. Combine all the vegetables in a bowl and mix in the oil, mustard, lemon juice and zest and stock. Spread over the chops and season well with salt and pepper. Bake for 40 minutes until all the vegetables are tender and the pork is cooked through.

To serve, spoon some of the vegetables onto each plate and place a chop on top. Garnish with chopped parsley.

Stir-fried Pork with Rainbow Vegetables and Hoisin Sauce

Serves 4

1 tablespoon canola oil
1 clove garlic, crushed
200 g lean pork fillet, thinly sliced
200 g broccoli, cut into florets
4 green onions, halved and cut into 3 cm lengths
1 medium carrot, peeled and thinly sliced
100 g snowpeas, trimmed and sliced on the diagonal
¼ red cabbage, finely shredded
2 tablespoons chopped brazil nuts or walnuts
⅓ cup hoisin sauce
½ cup chicken stock or water

Prepare all the vegetables and have everything to hand before you start cooking. Heat a wok or large frying pan over a medium heat and then add the oil. Toss in the garlic and pork and stir-fry for 2–3 minutes, then remove and set aside. Add the broccoli, green onions, carrot, snowpeas, cabbage, nuts, hoisin sauce and stock or water to the wok. Bring to the boil, tossing the vegetables until the cabbage has wilted and the broccoli and carrot are just cooked. Return the pork and garlic to the pan, and warm through.

Serve immediately, with boiled Doongara 'Clever Rice' or basmati rice.

Pork Roast with Balsamic Vinegar and Sweet Potato Mash

Serves 4–6

½ teaspoon freshly ground black pepper
1 teaspoon dried rosemary
2 teaspoons dark brown sugar
1 tablespoon olive oil
1 kg rolled loin of pork, trimmed of visible fat
2 red onions, cut into thin wedges
1 fennel bulb, trimmed and cut into thin wedges
150 ml balsamic vinegar
500 g sweet potato, peeled and cut into small pieces
a little skim milk
salt and freshly ground black pepper

Preheat the oven to 220°C.

Mix the pepper, rosemary, sugar and oil together, then rub over the pork. Place the onions and fennel in a baking dish and sit the pork on top. Pour over the balsamic vinegar, then bake for 20–25 minutes until everything is cooked through.

Meanwhile, put the sweet potato in a saucepan with enough water to cover, bring to the boil, cover and simmer for 5–7 minutes. Drain and mash with a little skim milk until smooth, seasoning well with salt and pepper.

Remove the pork from the oven and allow to rest for 15 minutes before carving. Serve with the sweet potato mash.

Butterflied Oriental Leg of Lamb

Serves 4–6

1 × 1.5 kg leg of lamb, butterflied out, trimmed of visible fat and
   thickest part of the meat scored with a knife

Marinade
1 clove garlic, crushed
1 teaspoon finely grated ginger
2 teaspoons ground coriander
1 teaspoon ground turmeric
2 tablespoons soy sauce
2 tablespoons white wine vinegar
1 tablespoon canola oil
freshly ground black pepper

Mix all the marinade ingredients together, rub over the
lamb, and leave to marinate for 1 hour.

Preheat the oven to 220°C and lightly grease a baking
dish. Skewer the lamb flat with two metal skewers, place
on the baking dish and bake for 45–50 minutes, or until
cooked through. Allow to rest for 20 minutes before
carving.

Serve with Yellow and Green Rice (page 69) and
chutney.

Moroccan Lamb Tagine with Fruit and Honey

Serves 6

1 kg lean cubed lamb, trimmed of all visible fat
1 tablespoon olive oil
1 teaspoon finely grated ginger
pinch of saffron threads (optional)
salt and freshly ground black pepper
½ teaspoon ground coriander
1 teaspoon ground cinnamon
1 large onion, finely chopped
100 g 'Craisins' (dried cranberries)
100 g dried apricots, diced
100 g dried prunes, pitted and roughly chopped
1 × 250 g packet frozen spinach, defrosted and drained
2 tablespoons honey
2 tablespoons chopped roasted almonds, for garnish

Place the lamb, oil, ginger, saffron (if using), salt and pepper, coriander, cinnamon and onion in a large saucepan. Cover with approximately 1½ litres of water, bring to the boil, then cover and simmer gently for about 2 hours, or until the lamb is tender. Add the dried fruit and cook for another 20 minutes. Stir in the spinach and honey, cook for a further 15 minutes, then taste and adjust seasoning if necessary.

Serve with Easy Couscous and Chickpeas (page 74) or basmati rice, garnished with chopped almonds.

A classic Moroccan tagine is given a pleasingly piquant flavour by the addition of 'Craisins' (dried cranberries). This is such an easy and tasty dish that it's worth making double the quantity and then freezing half for another time.

Slow-cooked Lamb Shanks with Parsnips and Red Onions

Serves 4

4 'Trim Lamb' shanks

¼ cup plain flour

1 tablespoon olive oil

2 red onions, peeled and quartered

2 cloves garlic, peeled but left whole

1 cup red wine

½ cup vegetable or chicken stock

2 tablespoons cider vinegar

8 parsnips, peeled and cut into chunks

2 bay leaves

1 strip lemon zest

salt and freshly ground black pepper

Preheat the oven to 180°C.

Coat the lamb shanks in the flour. Heat the oil in a frying pan and lightly brown the shanks on all sides, then transfer to a casserole dish. Fry the onion and garlic in the same pan for 3–4 minutes until browned, and then add to the casserole. Pour the wine into the frying pan to de-glaze, and bring to the boil. Pour over the lamb shanks, together with the stock and cider vinegar. Stir in the parsnips, bay leaves and lemon zest, and season well with salt and pepper. Cover the casserole, place in the oven and cook for about 1 hour, or until the lamb is very tender.

Serve with boiled basmati rice.

Lamb Loin with Niçoise Sauce

Serves 4

600 g lamb loin
salt and freshly ground black pepper
a little canola oil

Sauce
6 cloves garlic
1 × 400 g can diced tomatoes
½ cup kalamata olives, stoned and roughly chopped
2 cups frozen broad beans
3 cups frozen green beans
8 green onions, trimmed and thinly sliced
½ cup fresh basil leaves
3 tablespoons balsamic vinegar

Preheat the oven to 220°C.

Season the lamb and roll in a little olive oil. Place on a rack over a baking tray and cook in the oven for 10 minutes for medium rare, or about 15–20 minutes for well done. Remove and leave in a warm place to rest for 8 minutes.

Meanwhile, make the sauce. In a non-stick-frying pan, dry-fry the garlic in its skin over a medium heat for 3–4 minutes, until it begins to soften. Take the garlic cloves out of the pan, peel and slice into slivers. Heat the tomatoes, garlic and olives in a saucepan and gently cook for about 5 minutes. Add the frozen vegetables and green onions and cook for 4–5 minutes. Stir in the basil leaves and balsamic vinegar.

Serve with the sauce and mashed sweet potatoes.

Greek Baked Lamb and Eggplant Stacks

Serves 4

1 medium eggplant, cut into 12 rounds
1 tablespoon olive oil
1 onion, finely chopped
1 teaspoon dried oregano
½ teaspoon ground cumin
½ teaspoon ground cinnamon
300 g lean minced lamb
1 × 400 g can diced tomatoes
salt and freshly ground black pepper
4 tablespoons fresh wholemeal breadcrumbs
1 tablespoon dried parsley flakes

Grill the eggplant for 3–4 minutes each side in a chargrill pan or under a hot grill. Remove and cover with a tea towel. Heat the oil in a non-stick frying pan and gently fry the onion until soft, stir in the spices and lamb and cook for 5 minutes or until the meat is browned. Stir in the tomatoes and bring to the boil, simmer for 10 minutes, then remove from the heat and allow to cool a little. Season well with salt and pepper.

Preheat the oven to 180°C, and lightly grease a baking dish. Place four eggplant slices in the bottom of the dish and spoon a little sauce over each one. Continue alternating the eggplant and sauce until you have four three-layer stacks. Mix together the breadcrumbs and parsley and divide this topping between the stacks. Cover the dish with foil and bake for 30 minutes, then remove the foil and bake for a further 10 minutes. Serve immediately, accompanied by boiled Doongara 'Clever Rice'.

Canned products make a great standby. Research has demonstrated that canning actually protects against nutrient loss, so the fresh and the canned product are virtually identical in nutritional value.

Minted Lamb Cutlets with Cracked Wheat Pilaff

Serves 4

1 cup cracked wheat (burghul)
1¼ cups vegetable or chicken stock
2 tablespoons canola oil
1 large onion, finely chopped
salt and freshly ground black pepper
2 tablespoons finely chopped parsley
2 tablespoons finely chopped mint
8 lamb cutlets, trimmed of visible fat
4 tablespoons mint jelly
mixed salad leaves, to serve

Put the cracked wheat into a bowl and cover with the vegetable or chicken stock, then leave to stand for 45 minutes. Drain well, squeezing out as much liquid as possible. Heat 1 tablespoon of oil in a large frying pan, add the onion and cook for 3–4 minutes. Stir in the drained cracked wheat and cook for 4–5 minutes over a low heat, stirring all the time, until heated through. Season well with salt and pepper, then stir in the parsley and mint.

To cook the lamb, spread the mint jelly on both sides of the cutlets. Heat a chargrill pan or barbecue and cook the cutlets for 3–4 minutes each side.

Serve with the cracked wheat pilaff and a mixed-leaf salad.

Beef with Almonds

Serves 4

1 tablespoon canola oil
600 g rump steak, trimmed and cut into bite-sized cubes
1 tablespoon garam masala
20 g blanched almonds
2 teaspoons desiccated coconut
1 tablespoon finely grated ginger
2 cloves garlic, crushed
2 onions, finely chopped
100 ml water
200 ml plain low-fat yogurt
1 × 400 g can diced tomatoes
chilli paste
chopped parsley, for garnish

Heat the oil in a deep frying pan and brown the meat in small batches, then transfer to a flameproof casserole dish, leaving the oil behind. In the same pan, fry the garam masala, almonds and coconut until lightly browned, then spoon the mixture into a food processor. Add the ginger, garlic, onions and water, and blend into a smooth paste. Return the paste to the frying pan, and stir in half the yogurt and the tomatoes, adding chilli paste to taste. Pour the sauce over the meat, bring to the boil and then simmer gently for about ¾ hour, or bake in a 160°C oven, until the meat is tender. (It is important that this dish cooks at a low heat so that the yogurt does not curdle and the sauce thickens.)

Just before serving, spoon in the extra yogurt and stir through. Garnish with chopped parsley and serve with rice.

Musaman Beef Curry

Serves 4

1 tablespoon canola oil
500 g stewing steak (topside or rump), trimmed and cut into cubes
500 g small onions, peeled
or
500 g large onions, cut into quarters
1 large sweet potato (about 400 g), peeled and cut into small chunks
2 tablespoons Thai musaman curry paste
2 tablespoons coconut milk powder, mixed with 500 ml water
or
1 × 400 ml can light coconut milk, diluted with 100 ml water
2 tablespoons lemon juice
3 bay leaves
3 tablespoons brown sugar
freshly chopped coriander leaves, for garnish

In a large heavy-based saucepan, heat the oil and brown the
beef in batches. Remove with a slotted spoon and set aside.
Fry the onions and potato in the same pan, tossing until
lightly browned. Remove and set aside. Put the curry paste
into the pan and fry until fragrant, about 1 minute. Add the
coconut milk, bring to the boil and simmer for about
10 minutes. Return the beef, onions, and potatoes to the pan,
together with the bay leaves and brown sugar. Bring back to
the boil and simmer for about 20 minutes, or until beef is
tender and potatoes are cooked through.

Garnish with chopped coriander leaves and serve with
boiled basmati rice or Doongara 'Clever Rice'.

Silver Beet and Beef Rolls

Serves 4

400 g lean minced beef
25 g mushrooms, finely chopped
1 tablespoon red wine or beef stock
2 slices wholemeal bread, made into breadcrumbs
pinch of ground nutmeg
pinch of salt
½ teaspoon freshly ground black pepper
1 bunch silver beet (about 400 g)
1 × 400 g can diced tomatoes
juice of 1 lemon
¼ teaspoon dried basil

Mix together the beef, mushrooms, wine or stock, breadcrumbs, nutmeg, salt and pepper in a bowl. Remove coarse stalks from the silver beet, then plunge the leaves into a bowl of very hot water to wilt them; drain and pat dry. Make neat packages by carefully wrapping the silver beet leaves around meatball-sized quantities of the beef mixture. Place the packages in a large saucepan and add the tomatoes, lemon juice and basil. Cover and gently bring to the boil, then simmer for 45–50 minutes until cooked through.

Serve immediately, with boiled basmati rice.

A bowl of cherries (canned or fresh) makes a great way to boost your levels of the protective phytochemicals. These are found in all the darker fruits, including plums, cranberries and rhubarb.

desserts
& baking

Lemon Meringue Pie

Serves 6–8

6 sheets filo pastry
1 egg white, from an omega-enriched egg

Filling
1 × 400 g can skim sweetened condensed milk
4 egg yolks, from omega-enriched eggs
finely grated zest of 1 lemon
⅓ cup lemon juice
5 egg whites, from omega-enriched eggs
5–6 tablespoons castor sugar

Preheat the oven to 220°C, and lightly grease a 20 cm fluted pie tin.

Take one sheet of filo, fold in half and drape across the pie tin, then brush with egg white. Continue folding all the sheets, laying across the pie tin and brushing between the layers, until you have a firm base. Finish by brushing the base and side with egg white, then bake for 5 minutes until lightly browned. Remove and turn down the oven to 180°C.

To make the filling, mix the condensed milk, egg yolks, lemon zest and juice until well combined. Lightly beat the egg whites until fluffy, then gently fold 3 tablespoons of the egg whites into the lemon filling. Continue whisking the egg whites, gradually adding the sugar, until the mixture is stiff and glossy. Pour the lemon filling into the filo pastry shell, then carefully spoon the meringue over the top.

Bake for 20 minutes until the meringue is lightly browned and the filling is set. Remove and serve warm.

Egg white brushed onto a pastry pie shell before baking seals it, and stops it going soggy when the liquid filling is added. Use the leftover egg yolk in scrambled eggs, or make a batch of Almond Biscotti (page 156).

Maple-glazed Pear and Hazelnut Tart

Serves 6

olive oil spray
8 sheets filo pastry
juice of 1 lemon
¾ cup roasted hazelnuts, roughly chopped
½ cup maple syrup
6 canned pear halves, drained

Preheat the oven to 180°C, and lightly spray a baking sheet with olive oil.

Cut each sheet of filo pastry into three, to make 24 squares. Evenly space six filo squares on the baking sheet, squeeze a little lemon juice over the pastry, then sprinkle each square with some hazelnuts and drizzle over a little maple syrup. Repeat, adding layers of filo, hazelnuts and maple syrup, until all the filo is used (each tart should have four sheets of filo), but reserving some nuts and maple syrup for the topping. Thinly slice the pear halves and arrange on the filo tart cases. Sprinkle the reserved hazelnuts and maple syrup over the top. Bake for 35 minutes until the pastry is crisp and golden and the pears have caramelised.

Serve warm, with vanilla-flavoured yogurt or low-fat ice cream.

Baked Lemon Rice Pudding

Serves 4

⅓ cup Doongara 'Clever Rice' or pudding rice
½ cup castor sugar
1 litre low-fat milk
finely grated zest of 1 lemon
2 tablespoons flaked almonds

Preheat the oven to 175°C, and lightly grease a 2 litre baking dish.

Sprinkle the rice over the bottom of the baking dish. Combine the sugar and milk, and pour over the rice. Bake for about 1 hour, then stir in the lemon zest, sprinkle over the almonds and bake for a further 15–20 minutes. Remove and let stand for 10 minutes.

Serve warm with vanilla custard-style yogurt.

Milk contains a natural substance that promotes sleep. Bones are also better protected when there is a high calcium intake prior to bedtime. So go some milk, yogurt or custard in the evening for a sound night's sleep and strong bones.

Buttermilk Pancakes with Maple Syrup Apple Filling

Serves 4

4 omega-enriched eggs
225 ml buttermilk
1 tablespoon light olive oil
100 g plain flour
pinch of salt

Filling
3 tablespoons maple syrup
2 teaspoons ground cinnamon
1 × 310 g can apple chunks, drained
1 tablespoon roughly chopped pecan nuts

Combine the eggs, buttermilk and oil in a bowl, and lightly blend with a fork. Sift the flour and salt together. Slowly pour the wet ingredients into the dry and mix to make a smooth batter. Rest for 20 minutes while you make the apple filling. Warm the maple syrup and cinnamon in a pan over a gentle heat. Add the apples and pecans and stir for 1–2 minutes until they are warmed through.

To cook the pancakes, brush a little oil in a non-stick fry pan and heat over a medium heat. Pour in about ¼ cup of the batter and cook for 2–3 minutes each side. Keep warm, wrapped in a tea towel, until all the pancakes are done (this recipe should make about eight pancakes).

Place a spoonful of the filling in the middle of each pancake and fold over. Dust with icing sugar and serve warm, with honey-flavoured yogurt.

When stone fruit is in season, fill the pancakes with sliced fresh nectarines or plums.

Banana Bread Pudding

Serves 6

½ cup orange marmalade
3 thick slices of fruit bread
3 large firm bananas, peeled and cut into thick slices
4 large omega-enriched eggs, lightly beaten
1 litre (4 cups) low-fat milk
1 cup light brown sugar
1 tablespoon vanilla extract
1 teaspoon ground nutmeg
2 teaspoons ground cinnamon
icing sugar, for dusting

Preheat the oven to 180°C, and lightly grease a 2 litre ovenproof dish.

Spread the marmalade over the slices of bread, then cut into small chunks and lay half of them over the base of the prepared dish. Arrange the slices of banana over the bread, followed by the rest of the bread chunks. In a bowl, combine the eggs, milk, sugar, vanilla and spices. Pour over the bread and bananas. Cover the dish with foil and then place in a baking tray. Pour hot water into the tray to come halfway up the sides of the dish. Bake for 30 minutes, then remove the foil and bake for a further 30 minutes until the custard is firm and the top lightly browned.

Remove from the oven and allow to cool a little before dusting the top with icing sugar. Serve warm.

Italian Rice Tart

Serves 6

6 sheets filo pastry
1 omega-enriched egg white
1 litre low-fat milk
1 cup castor sugar
1 teaspoon vanilla extract
½ cup Doongara 'Clever Rice' or pudding rice
finely grated zest of 1 lemon
20 g currants
50 g fresh or frozen blackberries
icing sugar, for dusting

Preheat the oven to 220°C, and lightly grease a 20 cm flan tin.

Take one sheet of filo, fold in half and drape across the flan tin, then brush with egg white. Continue folding all the sheets, laying across the tin and brushing between the layers, until you have a firm base. Finish by brushing the base and side with egg white, then bake for 5 minutes until lightly browned. Remove and turn down the oven to 180°C.

Put the milk, sugar and vanilla into a saucepan and bring to the boil. Add the rice, bring back to the boil and then turn down the heat and simmer for 20 minutes. Transfer the rice mixture to a bowl, stir in the lemon zest, currants and blackberries and set aside to cool. When cold, spoon into the pastry case and bake on a preheated baking sheet for 30 minutes, until the filling is set and lightly browned on the top.

Leave to cool completely before cutting. Dust the top with icing sugar, and serve with a purée of strawberries or raspberries.

Pear, Ginger and 'Craisin' Crumble

Serves 6

12 canned pear halves, cut into small chunks
½ cup brown sugar
½ cup 'Craisins' (dried cranberries)
2 tablespoons plain flour
2 tablespoons orange juice
1 tablespoon finely chopped crystallised ginger
½ cup honey
⅔ cup rolled oats
⅓ cup finely chopped walnuts

Preheat the oven to 190°C, and lightly grease a 1 litre baking dish.

In a bowl, mix together the pears, sugar, 'Craisins', flour, orange juice and ginger and spoon into the baking dish. Heat the honey in a pan until runny, remove from the heat and stir in the oats and walnuts. Spoon the oat mixture over the pears and bake for 30 minutes, or until the crumble topping is crisp and golden.

Remove and allow to cool a little, before serving with vanilla-flavoured yogurt or custard.

Warm Upside-down Ricotta Puddings with Melba Sauce

Serves 6

12 shredded wheatmeal biscuits, crushed into crumbs
2 tablespoons honey
¼ cup reduced-fat cream cheese
1 cup low-fat ricotta
½ teaspoon vanilla extract
2 large omega-enriched eggs, lightly beaten
3 tablespoons castor sugar

Sauce
300 g canned or frozen raspberries (defrosted)
2 tablespoons redcurrant jelly
2 teaspoons icing sugar
1 tablespoon arrowroot, mixed with 1 tablespoon cold water

Preheat the oven to 175°C, and lightly grease a 6-cup jumbo muffin tin.

Combine the biscuit crumbs and honey and press into the bases of the muffin cups. Beat the cheeses, vanilla, eggs and sugar until smooth, then spoon evenly into the muffin cups. Bake for 20–30 minutes until set.

Meanwhile, make the Melba Sauce. Rub the raspberries through a sieve to remove all the seeds. Place the raspberry purée in a saucepan, add the redcurrant jelly and icing sugar, and slowly bring to the boil. Turn the heat down, stir in the arrowroot and simmer, stirring constantly, until the sauce has thickened (about 2–3 minutes).

Leave the puddings to cool for 10 minutes before turning out of the tin. Serve upside down, drizzled with the sauce.

Fruit and Nut Flan

Serves 6

6 sheets filo pastry
1 egg white, from an omega-enriched egg

Filling
3 omega-enriched eggs
50 g castor sugar
25 g hazelnuts, roughly chopped
25 g almonds, roughly chopped
25 g dried figs, roughly chopped
25 g pitted prunes, roughly chopped
25 g sultanas
1 tablespoon port or sherry
icing sugar, for dusting

Preheat the oven to 220°C, and lightly grease a 20 cm flan tin. Take one sheet of filo, fold in half and drape across the flan tin, then brush with egg white. Continue folding all the sheets, laying across the tin and brushing between the layers, until you have a firm base. Finish by brushing the base and side with egg white, then bake for 5 minutes until lightly browned. Remove and turn down the oven to 180°C.

Beat the eggs and sugar together until fluffy, then fold in the nuts, fruit and port. Pour into the flan base. Bake for 20–30 minutes on a preheated baking sheet until set.

Serve warm or cold, dusted with icing sugar, and with vanilla-flavoured yogurt on the side.

Baked Stuffed Apples

Serves 4

4 large apples (granny smith or golden delicious)
¼ cup rolled oats, lightly toasted in the oven
100 g dried dates, roughly chopped
50 g walnuts, roughly chopped
juice and finely grated zest of 1 lemon
25 g soft brown sugar
100 ml white wine or orange juice

Preheat the oven to 190°C, and lightly grease a shallow
baking dish large enough to hold the apples.

Core the apples and score the skin of each one around
its middle. Mix the oats, dates, nuts and lemon juice
and zest together. Spoon the filling into the apple cavities
and place in the prepared baking dish. Sprinkle over the
brown sugar, then pour in the wine or orange juice. Bake
for about 1 hour, basting with a little of the juices.

Serve warm or cold with vanilla-flavoured yogurt.

Sweet Potato and Orange Soufflé

Serves 4

500 g sweet potatoes
75 ml skim condensed milk
2 teaspoons finely grated orange zest
½ teaspoon baking powder
3 omega-enriched eggs, separated
2 tablespoons brown sugar
icing sugar, for dusting

Preheat the oven to 190°C, and lightly grease a 20 cm soufflé dish or four individual soufflé dishes.

Cut the sweet potatoes in half and place them skin side down on a lightly greased baking tray. Roast for about 30–40 minutes until soft. Scrape the flesh out of the skin into a bowl and mash. Mix in the condensed milk, orange zest, baking powder and egg yolks. In another bowl, whisk the egg whites until stiff and fold in the sugar, then carefully fold into the sweet potato mixture. Spoon into the soufflé dish and bake for 40 minutes, if using a large dish, or 20 minutes for individual soufflés.

Remove and serve immediately, dusted with icing sugar.

Frozen Almond and Fruit Terrine

Serves 8

150 g mixed dried fruit (peaches, mixed peel, raisins, currants)
¼ cup brandy, orange liqueur, sherry or orange juice
finely grated zest of 2 oranges
1 × 100 g bar almond brittle, broken into small pieces
300 ml vanilla-flavoured low-fat yogurt
3 egg whites, from omega-enriched eggs
200 g frozen strawberries or raspberries, defrosted

Soak the fruit in the brandy, liqueur, sherry or orange juice overnight.

Place the soaked fruit and its juices, orange zest, almond brittle and yogurt in a food processor and blend until smooth, then transfer the mixture to a bowl. Line a 500 ml loaf tin with non-stick baking paper. In a separate bowl, whisk the egg whites until stiff and fold through the fruit and nut mixture. Spoon into the prepared tin and place in the freezer. Leave for at least 3 hours or overnight. About 15 minutes before serving, transfer from the freezer to the fridge, and purée the frozen strawberries or raspberries with a little sugar to taste.

Rub a hot cloth across the bottom of the tin, turn the terrine out onto a chopping board and cut into serving slices. Spoon a little of the berry purée onto a plate and lay a slice of the terrine on top.

Fresh Lime Tart

Serves 6–8

4 tablespoons honey
1½ cups wheatmeal biscuit crumbs

Filling
1 × 400 g can skim sweetened condensed milk
4 egg yolks, from omega-enriched eggs
½ cup lime juice
grated zest of 1 lime
2 egg whites, from omega-enriched eggs
1 tablespoon castor sugar

Preheat the oven to 175°C and lightly grease a deep 20 cm
tart tin with a removable base.

Warm the honey until runny, stir in the biscuit crumbs
and press the mixture into the base and sides of the prepared
tin. Chill while you prepare the filling. Mix the condensed
milk with the egg yolks, lime juice and zest until well
combined. In a separate bowl, whisk the egg whites and
sugar until soft peaks form. Carefully fold through the lime
mixture until just incorporated. Pour the filling into the
prepared crust and bake for 40–50 minutes until filling puffs
up slightly.

Serve cold, with honey-flavoured yogurt or low-fat ice
cream.

This tangy lime filling can also be poured into 4 x 150 ml ramekin dishes and baked in a bain marie for 15 minutes until set. Serve cold, dusted with icing sugar and garnished with a few fresh blueberries or raspberries.

Keeping a tub of low-fat ice cream in the freezer means fruit and desserts can be served with a protective food. Not only is ice cream high in calcium, but a dairy product eaten at the end of the meal actually protects teeth against tooth decay and may even help control blood pressure.

Honey Grilled Peaches or Nectarines with Orange Ricotta Cream

Serves 4

8 ripe peaches or nectarines, halved and stones removed
½ cup honey
½ cup orange juice
1 tablespoon chopped glacé ginger
400 g low-fat ricotta
¼ cup plain low-fat yogurt
finely grated zest of 1 orange

Place the peaches or nectarines, cut side up, in a grill pan lined with non-stick baking paper. Heat the honey, orange juice and ginger in a saucepan until the honey is runny. Brush the nectarines with this syrup, reserving about 2 tablespoons. Allow the reserved syrup to cool before stirring into the ricotta, then mix in the yogurt and orange zest.

Grill the peaches or nectarines for 5–6 minutes until golden, and serve warm or cold with a dollop of the orange ricotta cream on top.

Apple and Rhubarb Crumble

Serves 4

350 g canned rhubarb
1 large apple, peeled, cored and cut into small chunks
¼ teaspoon ground cinnamon
pinch of ground nutmeg
2 tablespoons brown sugar
juice and finely grated zest of ½ lemon
1 loaf fruit bread, torn into small chunks (about 3 cups)
½ cup honey

Preheat the oven to 200°C, and lightly grease a shallow baking dish.

Mix the rhubarb, apple, cinnamon, nutmeg, sugar, lemon juice and zest together. Spread a third of the bread over the base of the baking dish, and spoon over half of the fruit mixture. Spread over another third of the bread and spoon over the rest of the fruit mixture, ending with the final third of the bread. Heat the honey in a saucepan until runny, then pour over the bread. Bake for 10–15 minutes, or until the apple is soft and the topping is crisp.

Serve warm with low-fat ice cream or vanilla-flavoured yogurt.

Hazelnut and Lemon Cake

Serves 6–8

3 large omega-enriched eggs, separated
100 g soft brown sugar
3 tablespoons plain low-fat yogurt
160 g hazelnuts (or almonds or pecans),
    roasted and ground into coarse crumbs
finely grated zest of 1 lemon

Preheat the oven to 180°C, and line a 23 cm springform cake tin with non-stick baking paper.

In a mixing bowl, whisk together the egg yolks and sugar until light and fluffy, then stir in the yogurt, nuts and lemon zest.

In another bowl, whisk the egg whites until stiff. Fold the egg whites into the egg yolk mixture very gently, then spoon into the cake tin and bake for about 35 minutes. (Test after 30 minutes by putting a skewer in the centre of the cake; if it comes out clean, the cake is done.)

When the cake has cooled, dust with icing sugar and serve with honey-flavoured yogurt and canned or fresh fruit.

Apricot Parfait

Serves 4

250 g dried apricots
juice and finely grated zest of 1 lemon
2 tablespoons sugar, or to taste
3 egg whites, from omega-enriched eggs

Soak the apricots overnight in water just to cover. Place the apricots and their soaking liquid in a saucepan, then add the lemon juice and zest and sugar to taste. Bring to the boil and simmer for 8 minutes until the apricots are soft, then whiz the apricots in a food processor until smooth. Set aside to cool.

Whisk the egg whites until stiff, then carefully fold in the apricot purée, a little at a time, until it is all incorporated. Spoon into individual dishes and serve with Almond Biscotti (page 156) and honey-flavoured yogurt.

This parfait freezes very well:
just pour into a lightly oiled loaf tin.
And for a change use other dried
fruits, such as apples, peaches,
or pears.

Almond Biscotti

Makes about 30 biscotti

250 g plain flour
250 g castor sugar
2 omega-enriched eggs, plus 1 extra egg yolk
1 teaspoon baking powder
¼ teaspoon salt
finely grated zest of ½ lemon
½ teaspoon vanilla extract
¼ teaspoon almond essence
100 g roasted almonds, roughly chopped

Preheat the oven to 180°C, and lightly grease a baking sheet.

Put all the ingredients except the almonds in a food processor, and process until the dough gathers into a ball. Remove and knead on a floured surface, folding in the nuts as you go. Divide the dough into two and shape each half into a log, then flatten slightly. Bake for about 20–30 minutes until lightly browned, then turn the oven down to 130°C. Remove the biscotti logs from the oven, allow to cool slightly, then cut crosswise into thin slices with a serrated knife. Spread out the biscotti on the baking sheet and return to the oven for a further 15–20 minutes to dry out. Remove and cool on a wire rack.

Store in an airtight tin.

Exotic Banana and Mango Parfait

Serves 4

1 large egg white, from an omega-enriched egg
150 g castor sugar
2 ripe bananas, peeled and sliced
125 ml pineapple juice
75 ml plain low-fat yogurt
50 g dried mango, chopped

Whisk the egg white until thick and foamy, gradually adding 2 tablespoons of the sugar; continue whisking until thick and shiny. Place the bananas, the rest of the sugar and the pineapple juice in a blender and whiz for about 15 seconds. Transfer to a bowl, fold in the egg white mixture and the low-fat yogurt and then stir in the mango. Pour into individual moulds and freeze overnight.

Remove from the freezer, unmould, and serve with Almond Biscotti (opposite) and honey-flavoured yogurt.

The traditional bacteria in yogurts are slightly different to those found in the human gut. So the newer yogurts using human-recognised bacteria, such as lactobacillus GG, are more likely to stay in the gut.

index

almonds
  Almond biscotti 156
  Beef with almonds 131
  Frozen almond and fruit terrine
    149
  Fruit and nut flan 146
  Stuffed cabbage leaves with rice
    and almonds 66
anchovies
  Rice-stuffed tomatoes with olives
    and basil 65
anti-oxidants 10–13
apples
  Apple and rhubarb crumble 153
  Baked stuffed apples 147
  Buttermilk pancakes with maple
    syrup apple filling 140–1
  Pork stuffed with apple and sage
    served with root vegetable bake
    118–19
apricots, dried
  Apricot parfait 155
  Moroccan lamb tagine with fruit
    and honey 124
  Spicy rice with grilled vegetables
    71

Aromatic coconut rice 68
Asian chicken salad 49
asparagus
  Chargrilled summer vegetable
    salad with white beans and herb
    dressing 40
  Prawn and spring vegetable risotto
    64
avocado
  Asian chicken salad 49
  Prosciutto and kidney bean salad
    41

Baked lemon rice pudding 139
Baked stuffed apples 147
bananas
  Banana bread pudding 142
  Exotic banana and mango parfait
    157
Barbecued fish on Asian cabbage
    salad 42
barley
  Mushroom and pearl barley soup
    29
basic ingredients 2–3
bean sprouts

Asian chicken salad   49
Crab and cabbage salad with soy
   dressing   47
beans   12
beans, cannellini
   Cannellini bean and eggplant
      gratin   88
   Chargrilled summer vegetable
      salad with white beans and herb
      dressing   40
   Steamed ling fillets with red
      capsicum sauce and mashed
      cannellini beans   98–9
beans, green
   Cashew nut curry   83
   Grilled marinated tuna or sword-
      fish with lentil salad and rocket
      38–9
   Easy spring vegetable pasta   52
   Lamb loin with Niçoise sauce   127
   Prawn and spring vegetable risotto
      64
   Thai chicken and vegetable curry
      114
beans, kidney
   Kidney bean, corn and spinach
      soup   30
   Mexican bean soup   27
   Prosciutto and kidney bean salad
      41
beef
   Beef with almonds   131
   Musaman beef curry   132
   Silver beet and beef rolls   133
   Thai beef salad in lettuce cups   46
beetroot
   Pasta with fresh herbs, lemon and
      roast vegetables   54
biscotti
   Almond biscotti   156
blackberries
   Italian rice tart   143

broccoli
   Cashew nut curry   83
   Chinese broccoli stir-fry with tuna
      104
   Stir-fried pork with rainbow
      vegetables and hoisin sauce   121
burgers
   Cheesy mushroom burgers   34
   Chicken-burgers on wholegrain
      rolls   35
Buttermilk pancakes with maple
   syrup apple filling   140–1

cabbage
   Barbecued fish on Asian cabbage
      salad   42
   Crab and cabbage salad with soy
      dressing   47
   Stir-fried pork with rainbow
      vegetables and hoisin sauce   121
   Stuffed cabbage leaves with rice
      and almonds   66
calcium   13, 139, 151
capsicums
   Chargrilled summer vegetable
      salad with white beans and herb
      dressing   40
   Chicken kebabs with Caribbean
      sauce   113
   Fresh mango and capsicum salsa
      with tuna   19
   Greek lentil salad with red
      capsicums, red onions and feta
      48
   Italian vegetable gateau   84
   Lentil and vegetable moussaka
      92–3
   Mexican corn pudding   87
   Moroccan chicken with 'Craisin'
      couscous salad   72–3
   Pasta with fresh herbs, lemon and
      roast vegetables   54

Prosciutto and kidney bean salad
  41
Rainbow pasta bake 55
Roast capsicum and tomato relish
  16
Spicy rice with grilled vegetables
  71
Steamed ling fillets with red
  capsicum sauce and mashed
  cannellini beans 98–9
Thai chicken and vegetable curry
  114
Vegetable tikka 80
carbohydrates 4–7
carrots
  Indian vegetable pancakes 86
  Potato, carrot and feta pancake
    stack with tomatoes 91
  Stir-fried pork with rainbow
    vegetables and hoisin sauce
    121
  Thai chicken and vegetable curry
    114
  Whole baked fish with pecan
    couscous 106–7
  Winter vegetable and tempeh
    casserole 81
cashew nuts
  Cashew nut curry 83
  Cracked wheat pilaff with pumpkin
    and cashew nuts 85
Chargrilled summer vegetable salad
  with white beans and herb
  dressing 40
cheese
  Cannellini bean and eggplant
    gratin 88
  Cheesy mushroom burgers 34
  Easy lasagne 56–7
  Italian vegetable gateau 84
  Rainbow pasta bake 55
  Risotto primavera 62

Salmon pies with cheese and corn
  105
Sicilian silver beet pizza 59
Sweet potato and feta frittata
  79
cherries 134
chicken 110–17
  Asian chicken salad 49
  Chicken-burgers on wholegrain
    rolls 35
  Chicken empanadas 22
  Chicken, feta and leek strudels
    112
  Chicken kebabs with Caribbean
    sauce 113
  Lemony chicken with raisins and
    chickpeas 117
  Moroccan chicken with 'Craisin'
    couscous salad 72–3
  Parcels of chicken with lime and
    sweet potatoes 110–11
  Roast chicken breasts with
    macadamia and waterchestnut
    stuffing 115
  Spicy summer chicken 116
  Thai chicken and vegetable curry
    114
  Thai-style chicken salad in lettuce
    cups 44
chickpeas
  Chickpea omelette rolls with
    cucumber, tomato and yogurt
    salad 32–3
  Chilli chickpeas with a couscous
    crust 82
  Easy couscous and chickpeas 74
  Lemony chicken with raisins and
    chickpeas 117
  Madras pork wraps with yogurt
    and mint 31
Chinese broccoli stir-fry with tuna
  104

corn
  Barbecued fish on Asian cabbage
    salad 42
  Chicken kebabs with Caribbean
    sauce 113
  Crab, corn and sweet potato cakes
    23
  Kidney bean, corn and spinach
    soup 30
  Rainbow pasta bake 55
  Salmon pies with cheese and corn
    105
  Sweet potato, pumpkin and corn
    chowder 28
cornbread
  Black olive cornbread 36
cornmeal
  Italian vegetable gateau 84
  Mexican corn pudding 87
couscous 72–5
  Chilli chickpeas with a couscous
    crust 82
  Easy couscous and chickpeas 74
  Moroccan chicken with 'Craisin'
    couscous salad 72–3
  Spicy lamb and couscous salad 75
  Whole baked fish with pecan
    couscous 106–7
Crab and cabbage salad with soy
  dressing 47
Crab, corn and sweet potato cakes
  23
cracked wheat see wheat, cracked
cranberries, dried ('Craisins')
  Curried rice, beans and vegetable
    pilaff 70
  Moroccan chicken with 'Craisin'
    couscous salad 72–3
  Moroccan lamb tagine with fruit
    and honey 124
  Pear, ginger and 'Craisin' crumble
    144

crumbles
  Apple and rhubarb crumble
    153
  Pear, ginger and 'Craisin' crumble
    144
cucumber
  Crab and cabbage salad with soy
    dressing 47
  Chickpea omelette rolls with
    cucumber, tomato and yogurt
    salad 32–3
  Spicy lamb and couscous salad
    75
  Tsatziki 17
curries
  Cashew nut curry 83
  Curried rice, beans and vegetable
    pilaff 70
  Musaman beef curry 132
  Thai chicken and vegetable curry
    114
dates see dried fruit
  Baked stuffed apples 147

desserts 136–57
dips
  Spicy sweet potato and tofu dip
    18
  Tsatziki 17
dressings
  Chargrilled summer vegetable
    salad with white beans and herb
    dressing 40
  Crab and cabbage salad with soy
    dressing 47
  Seared tuna with caperberry
    dressing 102

eggplant
  Cannellini bean and eggplant
    gratin 88
  Chargrilled summer vegetable

salad with white beans and herb dressing 40
Easy lasagne 56–7
Greek baked lamb and eggplant stacks 128–9
Italian vegetable gateau 84
Lentil and vegetable moussaka 92–3
Pasta with fresh herbs, lemon and roast vegetables 54
Spicy rice with grilled vegetables 71
Vegetable tikka 80
empanadas, Chicken 22

fats and oils 8–11
fennel
Lentil and vegetable pasta with crispy prosciutto 58
Pork roast with balsamic vinegar and sweet potato mash 122
Roast pork chops with mustard vegetables 120
feta
Chicken, feta and leek strudels 112
Greek lentil salad with red capsicums, red onions and feta 48
Potato, carrot and feta pancake stack with tomatoes 91
Sweet potato and feta frittata 79
figs
Fruit and nut flan 146
fish *see* seafood
flans and tarts
Fresh lime tart 150
Fruit and nut flan 146
Italian rice tart 143
Maple-glazed pear and hazelnut tart 138
folate 69

frittata, sweet potato and feta 79
fritters, prawn and green onion 101
Frozen almond and fruit terrine 149
Fruit and nut flan 146

glycemic index 5–7
Greek baked lamb and eggplant stacks 128–9
Greek lentil salad with red capsicums, red onions and feta 48
Grilled marinated tuna or swordfish with lentil salad and rocket 38–9

hazelnuts
Fruit and nut flan 146
Hazelnut and lemon cake 154
Maple-glazed pear and hazelnut tart 138
Honey grilled peaches or nectarines with orange ricotta cream 152

Indian vegetable pancakes 86
Italian rice tart 143
Italian vegetable gateau 84

kebabs, chicken, with Caribbean sauce 113
Kidney bean, corn and spinach soup 30

lamb
Butterflied oriental leg of lamb 123
Greek baked lamb and eggplant stacks 128–9
Lamb loin with Niçoise sauce 127
Minted lamb cutlets with cracked wheat pilaff 130

Moroccan lamb tagine with fruit and honey 124

Slow-cooked lamb shanks with parsnips and red onions 126

Spicy lamb and couscous salad 75

lasagne, easy 56–7

leeks
Chicken, feta and leek strudels 112

Risotto primavera 62

lemons
Baked lemon rice pudding 139

Hazelnut and lemon cake 154

Lemon meringue pie 136

Lemon pilau rice 67

Lemony chicken with raisins and chickpeas 117

lentils
Greek lentil salad with red capsicums, red onions and feta 48

Grilled marinated tuna or swordfish with lentil salad and rocket 38–9

Lentil and tomato soup with feta 26

Lentil and vegetable moussaka 92–3

Lentil and vegetable pasta with crispy prosciutto 58

Madras pork wraps with yogurt and mint 31

Pecan and lentil paté 20

limes
Fresh lime tart 150

Parcels of chicken with lime and sweet potatoes 110–11

Steamed fish with rice noodles and lime and sweet chilli sauce 96

linseeds 60

macadamia nuts
Roast chicken breasts with macadamia and waterchestnut stuffing 115

Madras pork wraps with yogurt and mint 31

mangoes
Exotic banana and mango parfait 157

Fresh mango and capsicum salsa with tuna 19

Prawn and rice salad with fresh mango 50

Thai-style chicken salad in lettuce cups 44

Maple-glazed pear and hazelnut tart 138

Mexican bean soup 27

Mexican corn pudding 87

Minted lamb cutlets with cracked wheat pilaff 130

miso 20

Moroccan chicken with 'Craisin' couscous salad 72–3

Moroccan lamb tagine with fruit and honey 124

moussaka, lentil and vegetable 92–3

Musaman beef curry 132

mushrooms
Cheesy mushroom burgers 34

Mushroom and pearl barley soup 29

Mushroom, spinach and tofu strudel 90

Roast mushrooms with pine nuts 21

Silver beet and beef rolls 133

Winter vegetable and tempeh casserole 81

nectarines
  Honey grilled peaches or
    nectarines with orange ricotta
    cream 152
noodles
  Asian chicken salad 49
  Steamed fish with rice noodles and
    lime and sweet chilli sauce 96
  Thai beef salad in lettuce cups 46
nutrition 1–13
nuts 12, 83; *see also* almonds,
    cashew nuts, hazelnuts,
    macadamia nuts, pecan nuts,
    pine nuts *and* walnuts

olives
  Black olive cornbread 36
  Easy lasagne 56–7
  Greek lentil salad with red
    capsicums, red onions and feta
    48
  Mexican corn pudding 87
  Lamb loin with Niçoise sauce 127
  Rice-stuffed tomatoes with olives
    and basil 65
omega-3 fats 8–10, 60
  omega-enriched eggs 23
omelettes
  Chickpea omelette rolls with
    cucumber, tomato and yogurt
    salad 32–3
oranges
  Orange ricotta cream 152
  Sweet potato and orange soufflé
    148
oxidation and anti-oxidants 11–13

pancakes
  Buttermilk pancakes with maple
    syrup apple filling 140–1
  Indian vegetable pancakes 86
  Potato, carrot and feta pancake

    stack with tomatoes 91
papaya
  Asian chicken salad 49
parfaits
  Apricot parfait 155
  Exotic banana and mango parfait
    157
parsnips
  Roast pork chops with mustard
    vegetables 120
  Slow-cooked lamb shanks with
    parsnips and red onions 126
  Winter vegetable and tempeh
    casserole 81
pasta 52–58
  Easy spring vegetable pasta 52
  Fishy pasta bake with prosciutto
    53
  Lentil and vegetable pasta with
    crispy prosciutto 58
  Pasta with fresh herbs, lemon and
    roast vegetables 54
  Rainbow pasta bake 55
paté, pecan and lentil 20
peaches
  Honey grilled peaches or
    nectarines with orange ricotta
    cream 152
  Spicy summer chicken 116
pears
  Maple-glazed pear and hazelnut
    tart 138
  Pear, ginger and 'Craisin' crumble
    144
peas
  Cashew nut curry 83
  Easy spring vegetable pasta 52
  Prawn and spring vegetable risotto
    64
  Risotto primavera 62
  Thai chicken and vegetable curry
    114

Winter vegetable and tempeh
  casserole 81
pecan nuts
  Parcels of chicken with lime and
    sweet potatoes 110–11
  Pecan and lentil paté 20
  Pork stuffed with apple and sage
    served with root vegetable bake
    118–19
  Spicy rice with grilled vegetables
    71
  Twice-baked sweet potatoes 94
  Whole baked fish with pecan
    couscous 106–7
phytochemicals 73, 134
phytoestrogens 26, 89
pies
  Lemon meringue pie 136
  Salmon pies with cheese and corn
    105
  Spicy fish and sweet potato pies
    100 ↖
pine nuts, with roast mushrooms
  21
pizza, Sicilian silver beet 59
polenta see cornmeal
pork
  Madras pork wraps with yogurt
    and mint 31
  Pork roast with balsamic vinegar
    and sweet potato mash 122
  Pork stuffed with apple and sage
    served with root vegetable bake
    118–19
  Roast pork chops with mustard
    vegetables 120
  Stir-fried pork with rainbow
    vegetables and hoisin sauce 121
potatoes
  Grilled marinated tuna or sword-
    fish with lentil salad and rocket
    38–9

Pork stuffed with apple and sage
  served with root vegetable bake
  118–19
Potato, carrot and feta pancake
  stack with tomatoes 91
Roast pork chops with mustard
  vegetables 120
Stir-fried squid with potatoes 108
Tempeh salad with new potoatoes,
  snowpeas and walnuts 45
prawns
  Prawn and green onion fritters
    101
  Prawn and rice salad with fresh
    mango 50
  Prawn and spring vegetable risotto
    64
prosciutto
  Fishy pasta bake with prosciutto
    53
  Lentil and vegetable pasta with
    crispy prosciutto 58
  Prosciutto and kidney bean salad
    41
protein foods 10–11
prunes
  Fruit and nut flan 146
  Moroccan lamb tagine with fruit
    and honey 124

puddings
  Baked lemon rice pudding 139
  Banana bread pudding 142
  Warm upside-down ricotta
    puddings with Melba sauce
    145
pumpkin
  Cracked wheat pilaff with pumpkin
    and cashew nuts 85
  Pork stuffed with apple and sage
    served with root vegetable bake
    118–19

Sweet potato, pumpkin and corn chowder 28

Rainbow pasta bake 55
raisins
Frozen almond and fruit terrine 149
Lemony chicken with raisins and chickpeas 117
raspberries
Frozen almond and fruit terrine 149
Warm upside-down ricotta puddings with Melba sauce 145
relish, roast capsicum and tomato 16
rhubarb
Apple and rhubarb crumble 153
rice
Aromatic coconut rice 68
Baked lemon rice pudding 139
Curried rice, beans and vegetable pilaff 70
Italian rice tart 143
Lemon pilau rice 67
Prawn and rice salad with fresh mango 50
Prawn and spring vegetable risotto 64
Rice-stuffed tomatoes with olives and basil 65
Risotto cakes 63
Risotto primavera 62
Spicy pilau rice with snapper fillets 97
Spicy rice with grilled vegetables 71
Stuffed cabbage leaves with rice and almonds 66
Yellow and green rice 69
ricotta
Honey grilled peaches or

nectarines with orange ricotta cream 152
Twice-baked sweet potatoes 94
Warm upside-down ricotta puddings with Melba sauce 145
risotto
Prawn and spring vegetable risotto 64
Risotto cakes 63
Risotto primavera 62
Roast capsicum and tomato relish 16
Roast chicken breasts with macadamia and waterchestnut stuffing 115
Roast mushrooms with pine nuts 21
Roast pork chops with mustard vegetables 120
rocket
Asian chicken salad 49
Grilled marinated tuna or swordfish with lentil salad and rocket 38–9

salads 38–50
Asian chicken salad 49
Barbecued fish on Asian cabbage salad 42
Chargrilled summer vegetable salad with white beans and herb dressing 40
Chickpea omelette rolls with cucumber, tomato and yogurt salad 32–3
Crab and cabbage salad with soy dressing 47
Greek lentil salad with red capsicums, red onions and feta 48
Grilled marinated tuna or swordfish with lentil salad and rocket 38–9

Moroccan chicken with 'Craisin'
   couscous salad   72–3
Prawn and rice salad with fresh
   mango   50
Prosciutto and kidney bean salad
   41
Spicy lamb and couscous salad
   75
Tempeh salad with new potoatoes,
   snowpeas and walnuts   45
Thai beef salad in lettuce cups   46
Thai-style chicken salad in lettuce
   cups   44
Tuna with roast sweet potato and
   spinach salad   43
salsas
   Fresh mango and capsicum salsa
      with tuna   19
seafood   96–108
   Barbecued fish on Asian cabbage
      salad   42
   Chinese broccoli stir-fry with tuna
      104
   Crab and cabbage salad with soy
      dressing   47
   Crab, corn and sweet potato cakes
      23
   Fishy pasta bake with prosciutto
      53
   Fresh mango and capsicum salsa
      with tuna   19
   Grilled marinated tuna or sword-
      fish with lentil salad and rocket
      38–9
   Prawn and green onion fritters
      101
   Prawn and rice salad with fresh
      mango   50
   Prawn and spring vegetable risotto
      64
   Salmon pies with cheese and corn
      105

Seared tuna with caperberry
   dressing   102
Spicy fish and sweet potato pies
   100
Spicy pilau rice with snapper fillets
   97
Steamed fish with rice noodles and
   lime and sweet chilli sauce   96
Steamed ling fillets with red
   capsicum sauce and mashed
   cannellini beans   98–9
Stir-fried squid with potatoes   108
Tuna with roast sweet potato and
   spinach salad   43
Whole baked fish with pecan
   couscous   106–7
Seared tuna with caperberry
   dressing   102
silver beet
   Sicilian silver beet pizza   59
   Silver beet and beef rolls   133
'slow' foods   5–7
Slow-cooked lamb shanks with
   parsnips and red onions   126
snowpeas
   Barbecued fish on Asian cabbage
      salad   42
   Stir-fried pork with rainbow
      vegetables and hoisin sauce   121
   Tempeh salad with new potoatoes,
      snowpeas and walnuts   45
soufflés
   Sweet potato and orange soufflé
      148
soups   26–30
   Kidney bean, corn and spinach
      soup   30
   Lentil and tomato soup with feta
      26
   Mexican bean soup   27
   Mushroom and pearl barley soup
      29

Sweet potato, pumpkin and corn
    chowder 28
soy beans
    Curried rice, beans and vegetable
        pilaff 70
    Easy lasagne 56–7
spinach
    Curried rice, beans and vegetable
        pilaff 70
    Kidney bean, corn and spinach
        soup 30
    Moroccan lamb tagine with fruit
        and honey 124
    Mushroom, spinach and tofu
        strudel 90
    Tuna with roast sweet potato and
        spinach salad 43
    Yellow and green rice 69
Steamed fish with rice noodles and
    lime and sweet chilli sauce 96
Steamed ling fillets with red
    capsicum sauce and mashed
    cannellini beans 98–9
stir-fries
    Chinese broccoli stir-fry with tuna
        104
    Stir-fried pork with rainbow
        vegetables and hoisin sauce 121
    Stir-fried squid with potatoes 108
strawberries
    Frozen almond and fruit terrine
        149
strudels
    Chicken, feta and leek strudels
        112
    Mushroom, spinach and tofu
        strudel 90
    Stuffed cabbage leaves with rice and
        almonds 66
sultanas
    Fruit and nut flan 146
sweet potatoes

Crab, corn and sweet potato cakes
    23
Curried rice, beans and vegetable
    pilaff 70
Lentil and vegetable moussaka
    92–3
Musaman beef curry 132
Parcels of chicken with lime and
    sweet potatoes 110–11
Pasta with fresh herbs, lemon and
    roast vegetables 54
Pork roast with balsamic vinegar
    and sweet potato mash 122
Pork stuffed with apple and sage
    served with root vegetable bake
    118–19
Roast pork chops with mustard
    vegetables 120
Spicy fish and sweet potato pies
    100
Spicy sweet potato and tofu dip
    18
Sweet potato and feta frittata
    79
Sweet potato and orange soufflé
    148
Sweet potato, pumpkin and corn
    chowder 28
Tofu and sweet potato cakes 89
Tuna with roast sweet potato and
    spinach salad 43
Twice-baked sweet potatoes 94
Vegetable tikka 80
Winter vegetable and tempeh
    casserole 81

tarts see flans and tarts
tempeh
    Tempeh salad with new potatoes,
        snowpeas and walnuts 45
    Winter vegetable and tempeh
        casserole 81

terrines
  Frozen almond and fruit terrine
    149
Thai beef salad in lettuce cups 46
Thai chicken and vegetable curry
    114
Thai-style chicken salad in lettuce
    cups 44
tofu 89
  Mushroom, spinach and tofu
    strudel 90
  Spicy sweet potato and tofu dip
    18
  Tofu and sweet potato cakes 89
tomatoes
  Cannellini bean and eggplant
    gratin 88
  Chicken kebabs with Caribbean
    sauce 113
  Chickpea omelette rolls with
    cucumber, tomato and yogurt
    salad 32–3
  Easy lasagne 56–7
  Lentil and tomato soup with feta
    26
  Lentil and vegetable pasta with
    crispy prosciutto 58
  Potato, carrot and feta pancake
    stack with tomatoes 91
  Rice-stuffed tomatoes with olives
    and basil 65
  Roast capsicum and tomato relish
    16
  Zucchini and semi-dried tomato
    slice 78
Tsatziki 17
tuna
  Chinese broccoli stir-fry with tuna
    104
  Fresh mango and capsicum salsa
    with tuna 19

Grilled marinated tuna or sword-
    fish with lentil salad and rocket
    38–9
Seared tuna with caperberry
    dressing 102
Tuna with roast sweet potato and
    spinach salad 43
Twice-baked sweet potatoes 94

vegetables
  Chargrilled summer vegetable
    salad with white beans and herb
    dressing 40
  Curried rice, beans and vegetable
    pilaff 70
  Easy spring vegetable pasta 52
  Indian vegetable pancakes 86
  Italian vegetable gateau 84
  Lentil and vegetable moussaka
    92–3
  Lentil and vegetable pasta with
    crispy prosciutto 58
  Pasta with fresh herbs, lemon and
    roast vegetables 54
  Prawn and spring vegetable risotto
    64
  Roast pork chops with mustard
    vegetables 120
  Spicy pilau rice with snapper fillets
    97
  Spicy rice with grilled vegetables
    71
  Thai chicken and vegetable curry
    114
  Vegetable bake 118–19
  Vegetable tikka 80
  Winter vegetable and tempeh
    casserole 81

walnuts
  Baked stuffed apples 147

Tempeh salad with new potatoes,
    snowpeas and walnuts   45
Warm upside-down ricotta puddings
    with Melba sauce   145
waterchestnuts
    Roast chicken breasts with
        macadamia and waterchestnut
        stuffing   115
wheat, cracked
    Cracked wheat pilaff with pumpkin
        and cashew nuts   85
    Minted lamb cutlets with cracked
        wheat pilaff   130
wheatgerm   78
wine, red   93
Winter vegetable and tempeh
    casserole   81

Yellow and green rice   69
yogurt   13, 33, 157
    Chickpea omelette rolls with
        cucumber, yogurt and tomato
        salad   115

zucchini
    Easy lasagne   56–7
    Indian vegetable pancakes   86
    Italian vegetable gateau   84
    Vegetable tikka   80
    Whole baked fish with pecan
        couscous   106–7
    Zucchini and semi-dried tomato
        slice   78

HIGH-CALCIUM COOKING

Jane Barnes & Syd Pemberton

Delicious recipes to boost your essential daily calcium intake

We all know that dietary calcium is vital for maintaining strong and healthy bones now, and for fending off osteoporosis in later life. But with the demands of a busy lifestyle, it can be hard to get your essential daily requirement.

High-Calcium Cooking shows you simple ways to boost your calcium levels, just by slurping on a smoothie or snacking on a yoghurt-based dip with crackers. The good news is that even a regular mid-morning cappuccino break can make all the difference!

Drawing on the latest research into calcium requirements for men, women and children, each recipe has a 'bone count', showing at a glance its calcium content.

Over 100 delicious, easy-to-follow recipes use a wide range of ingredients to help you create appetising meals that are rich in calcium and flavour – from Pistachio Nut and Ricotta Tart to Moroccan Fish Cakes, from luscious tapenades to decadent Chocolate and Orange Mousse.